Have Your Say ②

THIRD EDITION

Have Your Say  2

Listening and Speaking Skills and Practice

Irene S. McKay

George Brown College

OXFORD
UNIVERSITY PRESS

OXFORD
UNIVERSITY PRESS

Oxford University Press is a department of the University of Oxford.
It furthers the University's objective of excellence in research, scholarship,
and education by publishing worldwide. Oxford is a registered trade mark of
Oxford University Press in the UK and in certain other countries.

Published in Canada by
Oxford University Press
8 Sampson Mews, Suite 204,
Don Mills, Ontario M3C 0H5 Canada

www.oupcanada.com

First Edition published in 1999
Second Edition published in 2010

Library and Archives Canada Cataloguing in Publication
McKay, Irene, author
Have your say 2 : listening and speaking skills and practice / Irene S. McKay.—Third edition.

Accompanied by an audio CD.
ISBN 978-0-19-901171-1 (pbk.).—ISBN 978-0-19-901172-8 (CD)

1. English language—Textbooks for second language learners.
2. English language—Study and teaching (Higher)—Foreign speakers.
3. English language—Spoken English—Problems, exercises, etc.   I. Title.

PE1128.M1984 2015   428.3'4   C2014-907053-5

Cover image: © Rawpixel/Shutterstock

Oxford University Press is committed to our environment.
This book is printed on Forest Stewardship Council® certified paper
and comes from responsible sources.

Printed and bound in Canada

1 2 3 4 — 18 17 16 15

DEDICATION

For Samuel, John, Jocelyn, Ryan and Cassie, who have
brought love and laughter into my life.

AUTHOR ACKNOWLEDGEMENTS

I would like to thank all the ESL/EFL students I have taught, both at George
Brown College and in other contexts. Their struggles and successes in language
learning have provided me with insight and inspiration. I am also indebted to
the many ESL/EFL teachers I have trained. The amazing classroom experiences
I have had enabled me to produce this book. Working with and learning from
dedicated and conscientious learners has motivated me to produce materials
which I believe address learner needs and interests.

I also want to express my gratitude to all my friends and colleagues in ESL and EFL
for continuing to make the field of language teaching so stimulating and exciting.

I am deeply grateful to George Brown College for providing a fertile and
motivating environment for my work.

REVIEWERS

Oxford University Press Canada would like to express appreciation to the
instructors and coordinators who graciously offered feedback on *Have Your
Say 2* at various stages of the developmental process. Their feedback was
instrumental in helping to shape and refine the series.

Patricia Birch	Brandon University	Diane Mensch	Queen's School of English
Jessie Brown	Camosun College	Jane Merivale	Centennial College (formerly)
Lynne Bytyqi	University of Saskatchewan	Patrice Palmer	Mohawk College
Margaret Chell	Université de Montreal Gregory	James Papple	Brock University
		Carolyn Petersen	University of Saskatchewan
Shelagh Cox	Mount Royal University	Jeanne Robinson	Delview Adult Learning
Joan Dundas	Brock University		Centre (volunteer)
John Iveson	Sheridan College	Emily Rosales	Université de Québec à
Julian L'Enfant	Saint Mary's University TESL Centre		Montréal
		Mary Tang	Centennial College
Angela Losito	Université de Sherbrooke	Tony Vernon	Camosun College

Scope and Sequence Chart

CHAPTER	LISTENING Selections	SPEAKING			PRONUNCIATION
		Communication Focus	Grammar Skills		
1 GETTING ACQUAINTED— Giving Information and Descriptions	(1) The New Neighbour: A Conversation (2) Learning a New Language: An Interview	(1) Introducing yourself (2) Introducing others (3) Conversation openers—making small talk (4) Inviting (5) Describing personal characteristics (6) Complimenting (7) Handling problems in communication	• Simple present tense for facts and habits • The present progressive tense to express future plans		• Words with predictable stress patterns
2 TELLING IT AS IT WAS— Experiences and Achievements	(1) Farley Mowat, A Famous Canadian: A News Report (2) The Most Visited Places in the World: A Report	(1) Talking about past experiences, narrating (2) Encouraging conversation (3) Describing past habits (4) Explaining (5) Talking about similarities and differences (6) Paraphrasing	• The simple past tense • Past progressive tense • *Used to/would* expressing habitual actions in the past • Logical connectors— stating reasons: *because, because of, since, due to* • Logical connectors— stating results: *so, therefore, as a result* • Comparative and superlative forms of adjectives		• Pronunciation of regular past tense endings
3 EXPANDING NETWORKS— Friends, Families, and Relationships	(1) The Importance of Friendship: A Lecture (2) Canadian Families: A News Report	(1) Making requests using commands, modals, indirect questions, or hints (2) Responding to requests (3) Making requests using indirect questions/ statements (4) Asking for and giving information about present actions that started in the past (5) Getting time to think (6) Expressing necessity in the present (7) Expressing necessity in the past (8) Asking for and giving instructions to describe a process	• Modals used in requests: *can, will, could, would* • Indirect questions/ statements • Present perfect continuous (progressive) tense • *for* or *since* with the present perfect continuous (progressive) tense • Modals expressing necessity: *must, have to, have got to; had to*		• Intonation patterns for questions and statements

| CHAPTER | LISTENING Selections | SPEAKING | | PRONUNCIATION |
		Communication Focus	Grammar Skills	
④ **LIVING THE GOOD LIFE—** **Food and Lifestyles**	(1) Likes and Dislikes in Food: A Discussion (2) Exercise and Health: A CBC News Report	(1) Talking about events in the indefinite past (2) Expressing likes and dislikes (3) Stating opinions; agreeing, disagreeing and supporting opinions	• Present perfect tense for actions in the indefinite past • Verbs taking gerunds and infinitives	• Stressed and unstressed words
⑤ **THRILLS AND CHILLS—** **Leisure, Sports, and Entertainment**	(1) Extreme Sports: A Radio Interview (2) Is Violent Media Just Entertainment?: A Lecture	(1) Stating and asking about preferences (2) Expressing ability and inability (3) Expressing advisability (4) Regretting, reprimanding, and criticizing (5) Summarizing (6) Expressing possibility/ speculating (7) Expressing possibility in the past/speculating about past events	• *would rather/prefer* used to express preferences • Modals expressing ability: *Can/could* and *was/were able to* • Modals expressing advisability: *Should/ ought to/had better* • Modals: *should have* + past participle; *shouldn't have* + past participle • Modals expressing possibility: *might/may/ could* • Modals: *might have* + past participle; *may have* + past participle; *could have* + past participle	• Linking words in connected speech
⑥ **LISTENING TO YOUR HEAD AND YOUR HEART—** **Emotions and Work**	(1) Social Intelligence and Leadership: An Interview (2) Australia Flooded by Dream Job Applicants: A News Report	(1) Expressing assumptions and probability (2) Expressing assumptions and probability in the past (3) Expressing emotions (4) Making and responding to suggestions (5) Apologizing and responding (6) Giving complex descriptions (7) Adding information and ideas to maintain conversation (8) Describing skills, knowledge, and abilities (9) Interrupting	• Modals expressing probability: *must, can't, couldn't, mustn't* • Modals expressing probability in the past: *must have* + past participle; *can't have* + past participle; *couldn't have* + past participle, *mustn't have* + past participle • Adjectives and adjective clauses • Relative pronouns • Question words + infinitives	• More on linking

CHAPTER	LISTENING Selections	SPEAKING			PRONUNCIATION
		Communication Focus	Grammar Skills		
⑦ UNDERSTANDING DIFFERENCES— Society and Culture	(1) The Do's and Taboos of Body Language: An Interview (2) Copyright Laws: A Documentary Report	(1) Making recommendations and predicting consequences (2) Restating and hesitating (3) Making complaints (4) Expressing warnings and prohibitions	• Conditional sentences referring to future time • *recommend, suggest +* subjunctive • Modal expressing prohibition: *mustn't* • Modal expressing warning: *had better not*		• Information focus and intonation
⑧ RESPECTING OUR WORLD— Nature and the Environment	(1) Elephants in Zoos: A Radio Interview (2) The Effects of Climate Change on the Food Supply: A Documentary Report	(1) Using the passive voice to ask for and give impersonal information (2) Expressing disapproval and criticizing (3) Expressing opinions with various degrees of certainty (4) Expressing regrets (5) Hypothesizing	• The passive voice • *to be supposed to* • Using *wish* to talk about present, past, and future time • conditionals		• Non-final intonation and final intonation • Using intonation pattern to indicate choices • Intonation pattern with lists

Contents

CHAPTER 3

EXPANDING NETWORKS—Friends, Families, and Relationships   55

CHAPTER 4

LIVING THE GOOD LIFE—Food and Lifestyles   85

CHAPTER 5

CHAPTER 6

CHAPTER 7

UNDERSTANDING DIFFERENCES—Society and Culture   169

CHAPTER 8

RESPECTING OUR WORLD—Nature and the Environment   197

INTRODUCTION

Overview

Audience

Have Your Say 2 is a listening and speaking skills and practice text for high beginners in Intensive English, English for Academic Purposes, LINC, and other ESL programs. It is designed to take learners from Benchmark 3 to Benchmark 5 of the Canadian Language Benchmarks. It is the first book in a three-level course in listening and speaking.

Approach

Have Your Say 2 incorporates some of the popular features of the previous *Have Your Say* text such as pronunciation and vocabulary. It is based on the concept that learner-centredness and exposure to authentic, meaningful language in collaborative activities motivate learners and provide them with the means for developing proficiency in listening and speaking. As learners communicate orally, their confidence in their abilities to communicate increases, and this eventually leads to improved listening and speaking skills. The text provides scaffolding and activities to enable learners to expand their communicative competence.

Have Your Say listening and speaking activities provide the learners with meaningful tasks that give them a real reason to communicate verbally in English. There is a focus on both form and function. Learners are motivated to talk and share their experiences and feelings. The materials are constructed so that they can be a jumping-off point for further conversations. An important feature of the materials is that they help to foster an accepting atmosphere in the language classroom which makes learners feel secure, valued, and free to experiment with the language in expressing themselves. The activities provide variety in topics, groupings, language skills addressed, and task types to keep the learners engaged.

Features of the Text

Listening Sections

Each chapter contains two main listening sections. The content of each of the listening texts is related to the overall theme of the chapter. There is variety in the types of listening. Some are conversations of relevance to beginning-level learners. Others are short lectures, reports, and interviews, which prepare learners for longer listening texts. Since the goal of all listening activities is to prepare learners to eventually comprehend authentic listening materials, several selections are authentic radio or TV programs chosen for their comprehensibility and length to make them accessible to lower-level learners. It's important for English language learners to be exposed to authentic language, even at the lower levels.

Pre-listening Activities

Each main listening section is introduced by pre-listening activities. Some of these encourage top-down processing, which occurs when learners exploit their background knowledge to understand texts. These include speaking exercises; the use of pictures, quizzes, surveys; and other activities to engage the learners in thinking and talking about the topic and in this way to activate their background knowledge. Each listening section also contains activities to encourage bottom-up processing, which occurs when learners use their grammatical and lexical knowledge to aid comprehension. These include exercises focusing on the vocabulary used in the recording.

During-Listening Activities

There are two main kinds of during-listening activities: Listening for the Main Ideas asks the learners to understand the overall gist of the text, and Listening Comprehension requires the learners to listen for specific information in the text. Each listening selection has both types of activities.

Personalizing

The final activity for each listening selection is Personalizing, which engages the learners in analyzing or evaluating the information they heard and reacting to it.

Speaking Sections

Almost all ESL/EFL learners complain that they do not get enough speaking practice. *Have Your Say 2* provides a wide variety of speaking activities to involve learners as much as possible in using language meaningfully. Each chapter contains two main speaking sections, each of which includes a number of Communication Focuses. Speaking activities occur before and after the listening sections and impress upon learners the importance of oral communication skills.

Communication Focus

Each Speaking section begins with a Communication Focus; others occur as needed. The purpose of each Communication Focus is to introduce speech acts and language functions. They focus the learners' attention on certain language functions and encourage them to produce these during the speaking activities.

Speaking Activities

The speaking activities are linked to the theme of the chapter. They are related to and support the Communication Focus sections. Speaking activities appear in both the Listening and the Speaking sections. The speaking activities include interviews and questionnaires in which there is an information gap, partner and group activities in which the learners collaborate to reach a goal, short group and individual presentations, whole-class activities, communication games, and role plays. These activities are designed to encourage learners to produce a large quantity of language, which will eventually lead to improved speaking skills.

Grammar Notes

The Speaking sections often include one or more summaries of the grammatical structures the learners are encouraged to use during the chapter's speaking activities. The aim of the Grammar Notes is to encourage students to produce these structures at the same time as they are working on improving their fluency.

Listening and Speaking Strategies

Where relevant, various specific strategies primarily for developing listening and speaking skills appear in the margins throughout the chapters. Teachers can use these as jumping-off points both to discuss the strategies learners can use and to encourage learners to try to use new strategies to progress in their everyday communication.

Pronunciation Sections

Each chapter contains one or more pronunciation focuses—these may deal with segmentals (individual sounds) or suprasegmentals (features greater than individual sounds such as intonation). The pronunciation activities involve distinguishing and identifying a particular aspect of English pronunciation and then producing it. Learners are asked to practise pronunciation with each other in a variety of activities.

Communicating in the Real World

Each chapter contains a final section which asks the learners to take what they have learned and apply it beyond the classroom. Learners are asked to speak to people who are not in their classes, asking some of the questions they have been discussing in the chapter, and to then present their findings and experiences to the class. In some chapters, students can also work on projects and presentations which take them outside the classroom to extend their learning.

Self-Evaluation

When learners take responsibility for their learning, both language proficiency and strategy use increase. Each chapter ends with a self-evaluation section which allows learners to reflect on what they have accomplished and to consider where they need to improve and what they still need to learn. Students can complete these evaluations individually, or the sections can be used as the basis for journal writing or discussion.

CHAPTER 1

Getting Acquainted

Giving Information and Descriptions

Introducing yourself
Introducing others
Conversation openers—making small talk
Inviting
Describing personal characteristics
Complimenting
Handling problems in communication

THINKING AND TALKING

Work with a partner. Choose a picture. Describe the people in the picture. What are they doing? What do you think they are saying? How do you think they feel?

Tell your partner about the first time you came to this school. Who did you meet? How did you feel? How have your ideas changed since then?

LISTENING 1: THE NEW NEIGHBOUR— A CONVERSATION

Before You Listen

👥 Pre-listening Activity

1. Think about the last time you met someone new. Tell your partner where this took place. Who did you meet, and what did you learn about the person?

2. You will hear a conversation on the audio CD between two people who are meeting for the first time. Predict three pieces of information they will give about themselves.

   a. _____

   b. _____

   c. _____

👥 Pre-listening Vocabulary

A. You will hear a conversation on the audio CD that includes the following vocabulary. Work with a partner or by yourself to write the correct word next to its definition in the chart below.

reputation	sociable	teams	considerate	antique
nervous	creative	honest	couch	optimistic
supportive	artistic	cooperative	gorgeous	

Definitions	Vocabulary
1. opinions or beliefs people have about someone or something	reputation
2. a piece of furniture or art which is expensive because it is very old	
3. worried or afraid about something	
4. sofa	
5. very beautiful	
6. giving emotional help and encouragement	
7. friendly; liking to be with and talk to people	
8. being able to make new things or have new ideas	
9. having skill in art and in relating to art and beauty	
10. groups of people who play a sport against other groups	
11. positive, hopeful, expecting the best to happen	
12. working together with others	
13. telling the truth	
14. thinking about others and their feelings	

B. Choose the correct words from the list above to fill in the blanks in these sentences. Use each word only once. Not all the words are used in the sentences. Please make changes to verbs or nouns when necessary.

1. John is well known in the business community. He has an excellent _____reputation_____ for doing great work.

2. This table is over one hundred years old.
   Really? I guess it's an _____.

3. I have a job interview this afternoon, and I feel really _____ about it.

4. Mary Ann enjoys meeting people and interacting with them. She's very _____.

5. This is Alex. He takes wonderful photographs. Everyone say he is very _____ and _____.

6. I really love your new coat. It's _____.

7. Anna works well with _____ of people because she's very _____.

8. Teachers need to help students to do their best. They need to be _____ when the students are having a hard time.

9. My friend Allen always expects the best outcomes. He's very _____.

10. Helen always thinks about other people first. She's a very _____ person.

Listening for the Main Ideas

 Track 1   Listen to the conversation once, and then answer the questions.

1. Where are the speakers?
2. What are two topics they talk about?
3. Which of your predictions was correct?

Listening Comprehension

 Track 2   Listen to the conversation as many times as you need to. Complete the chart.

Man's name	
Woman's name	
What does she say about the students at the college?	
How does she get to the school?	
What are two things she does in the mornings?	
What does she offer to do?	
What information about the apartment building does she give him?	
What does she invite him to?	
What other things do they talk about?	

Personalizing

1. Tell your partner about the last time you moved. How did you feel about moving to a new place? How did you find out about the transportation and about the area?
2. Think about the conversation you just heard. In other countries, how do people introduce themselves and speak to each other when they meet for the first time? What body language do they use? What are some similarities and differences?

VOCABULARY AND LANGUAGE CHUNKS

Write the number of each expression next to its meaning. After checking your answers, choose six expressions and write your own sentences.

Expressions

1. to make friends
2. by the way
3. to take a lot of time
4. in no time
5. all set

Meanings

_____ to arrive
_____ very quickly
_____ to stay awake, not to go to bed
_____ to board
_____ to telephone someone

6. to stay up	_____	to await, to expect
7. to get up	__1__	to become friends
8. to get on	_____	ready
9. to get to	_____	incidentally; something we say to introduce a new subject or additional information
10. to give someone a call	_____	to like very much
11. in time	_____	just before a set time or deadline
12. to wait for	_____	to wake up and get out of bed
13. to be into	_____	to require a long time
14. to look forward to	_____	a great deal of, lots of
15. no big deal	_____	to invite people to your house
16. to have people over	_____	nothing very important
17. to drop by	_____	to call someone or go and talk to someone
18. tons of	_____	to think about something pleasant which will happen; to anticipate
19. to give someone a shout	_____	to go to someone's place without a formal invitation

SPEAKING 1

Communication Focus 1: Introducing Yourself

Structures/Expressions	Examples	Responses
Hello, my name is . . .	Hello, my name is Cassie.	Hello, Cassie.
Hi, I'm . . .	Hi, I'm Cassie.	Hi.
Hi, I'd like to introduce myself.	Hi, I'd like to introduce myself. My name is Ryan Thomas.	(It's) Nice to meet you.
Hi, I don't think we've met. I'm . . .	Hi, I don't think we've met. I'm Ryan Thomas.	(I'm) Glad to meet you. My name is Sarah.
Let me introduce myself. I'm . . .	Let me introduce myself. I'm Ryan Thomas.	I'm Sarah.

More Formal

Structures/Expressions	Examples	Responses
Hello, I don't believe we've met.	Hello, I don't believe we've met. I'm Helen Tang.	How do you do?
Allow me to introduce myself.	Allow me to introduce myself. My name is Bruce Ross.	Pleased to meet you.

👥 SPEAKING ACTIVITY 1

Work with a partner. Number the sentences in the following conversations in the correct order and then practise saying them. Choose one of the conversations as a model and make up a conversation to introduce yourselves. Role-play your conversation for the class.

Conversation A

_____   Hi, I'm Sheila. I'm glad to meet you.

_____   That would be great! Let's do that. We can have coffee or a drink and practise our English. I'm really glad we met.

_____   I think it's difficult but it's lots of fun. I'm having a ball doing the activities.

_____   It's nice meeting you, too. How are you finding the work in the English course?

_____   Maybe we can get together after class one of these days, compare notes, and share our ideas.

_____   It's keeping me busy. I enjoy it, but it's challenging. What about you?

_____   Hello, my name is Jackie. I'm in the same English class as you. I sit several rows behind you.

Conversation B

_____   Thanks for listening and for the advice.

_____   That's an excellent idea. I guess I need to make a complaint. Maybe there is a way to fix the problem.

_____   Pleased to meet you, Michael. I'm Diane Lawrence.

_____   Well, no, not really. I can't say that I do. What about you? Does the noise bother you, Michael?

_____   That's too bad. I'm sure there's a solution to it. Why don't you speak to the superintendent?

_____   Hello. Allow me to introduce myself. My name is Michael Rogers. I believe we live in the same building. I see you there all the time.

_____   Good luck!

_____   How do you do? I hope you don't mind if I ask you a question. Do you hear a lot of noise late at night in your apartment?

_____   Yes. It's a big problem for me. I hear the elevator and noises from the lobby. Sometimes the noise is so bad that I can't sleep.

👥 SPEAKING ACTIVITY 2

Introduce yourself to the class. Tell them three things about yourself, two of which are not true. The person who guesses which statement is true takes the next turn.

SPEAKING ACTIVITY 3

As a class, stand in two circles, one circle inside the other. If you are in the outside circle, move clockwise. If you are in the inside circle, move counter-clockwise. The teacher will play some music. When the music stops or when the teacher claps his or her hands, stop moving.

Face your classmates in the other circle, shake hands, introduce yourselves, and talk. After several minutes the music will start again. When the music starts, move around in your circles. The music will start and stop several times. At the end of 15–20 minutes, report about one or two of the people you met.

SPEAKING ACTIVITY 4

Work in a group of three. Discuss the expressions in the following list and put them into the correct categories. Some of these are expressions we use when we meet people. Others are expressions we use to say goodbye. There are also expressions we use when we want to get a person's attention. You can also talk about other expressions that you hear but which are not on the list. Put a plus sign (+) next to expressions that you think are more formal and a minus sign (−) next to those that you think are informal.

Hey!	What's up?	Have a good day.	Good afternoon.
Pardon me.	See you later.	Good evening.	Take care.
Hi there!	Good night.	Excuse me, can I ask a question?	How are things?
Good day.	So long.	Got a minute?	Long time no see!
Bye now.	Have a good one.	I'm sorry to bother you.	Keep in touch!
How's it going?	Talk to you soon.	Excuse me.	Good morning.

Greetings	Saying Goodbye	Getting Attention

Grammar Note: Simple Present Tense for Facts and Habits

We can use the simple present tense to talk about facts, habits, and routines.

When we talk about habitual activities, we often use adverbs or phrases such as *every day*, *every month*, *on Fridays*, *on Mondays*, *once in a while*.

We can also use adverbs of frequency, such as *always*, *never*, *often*, *sometimes*, *usually*, *frequently*, and *rarely*, with the simple present tense.
Examples:

> <u>Fact:</u> Sam, have you met Cecile? She comes from Uruguay.

> <u>Habit or routine:</u> This is Melinda. She usually goes jogging before she comes to school.

SPEAKING ACTIVITY 5

Work in a group of four. For each person, find out a fact and a habit. Report to the class about someone in your group.

	Me	Partner 1	Partner 2	Partner 3
Facts				
Habits				

Communication Focus 2: Introducing Others

Structures/Expressions	Examples
I would like to introduce . . .	George, I'd like to introduce Mathew. Mathew teaches photography.
I'd like you to meet . . .	Marta, I'd like you to meet Nicole. She speaks French.
Do you know . . .	Doug, do you know Ruby? She works in the registration office.
This is . . .	Laura, this is Edward. He has an interesting hobby. He collects coins from all over the world.

Speaking STRATEGY

When we introduce people to each other, we usually give some interesting information about them or point out something they have in common so that a conversation can begin.

SPEAKING ACTIVITY 6

Work with a partner to conduct interviews with each other. Form the questions and then find out the answers. Then join another pair of students and introduce each other. Give some important information about the person you are introducing.

Information	Questions	My Answers	My Partner's Answers
Name? Nickname?	What is your name? Do you have a nickname?		
Languages?			
Length of time in this city?			
Single/married?			
Length of time studying English?			
Reasons for taking this course?			
Previous travel/countries visited?			
Future plans/long term goals/ ambitions?			
Problems in learning English?			
Interests/hobbies/sports?			
Education/number of years/ majors/degrees?			
Other question(s)?			

SPEAKING ACTIVITY 7

Work in a group of four. List all the things you have in common (things that are the same about you). List all your differences. Think about habits, likes, dislikes, interests, family, and opinions. You can also think about favourites—foods, places, activities, music, etc. The group which finds the most similarities and differences wins!

SPEAKING ACTIVITY 8

Work with a partner. Each of you will imagine the person you would like to be in the future. This person is going to make a speech or presentation at a conference or business meeting. Interview your partner and fill in the chart.

Introduce the person your partner would like to be to the class. Make sure you include lots of interesting details in your introduction.

	Me	My Partner
Name		
Profession		
Nationality		
Accomplishment		
Hobbies/interests		
Topic of presentation/speech		

Communication Focus 3:
Conversation Openers—Making Small Talk

People often make small talk to start a conversation. The topics for small talk are general and impersonal, such as the weather, sports, a compliment, or a general comment about something the speakers have in common. Look at the following examples.

Structures/Expressions	Responses
Wonderful weather we're having!	Yes. It feels like spring.
What rotten weather!	I know. It's really snowing hard.
Are you enjoying the party?	Yes I am. The people are very nice.
Are you new to the class?	Yes. I just registered yesterday.
That's a fabulous umbrella. Can I ask where you got it?	Thanks. There was a sale at The Umbrella Shop just last week, and I bought it then.

SPEAKING ACTIVITY 9

Work with a partner. Write *yes* if you think the following openers are appropriate and *no* if you think they are not appropriate. Decide where you could use the appropriate openers.

Openers	Appropriate?	Responses	Locations
Hot enough for you?			
Having a good time?			
What terrible weather we're having!			
Boy this elevator is slow!			
I heard that you failed the test.			
Is the bus running on time?			
Are you a foreigner?			
Where do you live?			
You look different. Did you put on a lot of weight?			
Great dog! Is he a lot of trouble to look after?			
What a nice jacket! How much did you pay for it?			

👥 SPEAKING ACTIVITY 10

Work with a partner. Think of openers and responses to use in the following situations. Then role-play a small-talk conversation for the class. Ask the class to guess the situation.

1. You are waiting for the elevator.
2. You are waiting for your fitness class at the gym.
3. You are at a park.
4. You are at a party.
5. You are looking for a grammar book in a bookstore.
6. Other:

SPEAKING 2

Communication Focus 4: Inviting

Extending Invitations

Structures/Expressions	Examples
Would you like to . . .	I'm having some people over for pizza after school tomorrow. Would you like to join us?
Do you feel like . . .	Are you hungry? Do you feel like going out for something to eat after class?
How about . . .	Are you doing anything on Saturday? How about going out to a movie?

Replying

Accepting
I'd love to.
That would be nice.
That's a great idea. I would really like to.

Refusing and Making Excuses
I'd like to, but I can't. I'm babysitting. Maybe we can get together some other time?
I'm afraid I can't. I have to study for an important test.
I would really like to, but I'm busy. My sister is coming over.

IS IT REALLY AN INVITATION?

Many English speakers will use expressions such as the following:

Let's get together some time!

Why don't we go out after school one of these days?

Why don't you drop by sometime?

We should have dinner soon.

These are **NOT** invitations. These are just expressions of liking and admiration. A true invitation usually includes a specific date and time.

Grammar Note: The Present Progressive Tense to Express Future Plans

In English, we use the present progressive tense for an action in progress.
Example:

> I am studying English now.

We can also use the present progressive tense to express future plans. When we use the present progressive tense in this way, we need to have a future time reference in the sentence.
Examples:

> I am going on vacation <u>in two weeks</u>.
>
> What are you doing <u>next summer</u>?
>
> They are going out <u>tomorrow night</u>.

 SPEAKING ACTIVITY 11

Walk around the room and invite a different person to four of the following activities which appeal to you. Other people will invite you to other activities. Respond honestly. Accept and turn down invitations.
Examples:

> I'm having some people over to play Scrabble tomorrow. Would you like to join us?
>
> My friend and I are going swimming next Saturday. Do you feel like coming with us?

1. Go to a movie (choose a specific time and date)
2. Go shopping (choose a specific place)
3. Have dinner in a restaurant (choose a specific one)
4. Have coffee at a café (choose a specific one)
5. Go to a basketball game
6. Go to a museum
7. Go to a karaoke bar
8. Go for a walk (choose a specific place)
9. Go skating
10. Go hiking
11. Go to a play or concert

Communication Focus 5: Describing Personal Characteristics

We often use adjectives to describe people or things. Sometimes we give an example or an explanation.

Adjectives	Examples
outgoing	Sonia is outgoing. She is usually the life of the party.
quiet/shy/reserved	Jason is quiet, shy, and reserved. He doesn't like going to parties.
cautious	Paul is cautious. He always checks his answers.
ambitious	Michelle is ambitious. She wants to be the president of a bank.
optimistic	Barack is optimistic. He never believes that anything bad will happen.
adventurous	Anita is adventurous. She always wants to go to new places and meet new people.
eager	Helen is eager to improve her English. She studies and practises all the time.
persistent	James is very persistent about finding a job. He sends out resumés all the time. He doesn't give up.
impulsive	Kim is impulsive. She often buys things on the spur of the moment, without thinking very long.
confident	Dave is very confident. He believes everyone wants to be his friend.
energetic	Linda is energetic. She does twice as much as anyone I know.

SPEAKING ACTIVITY 12

Use three adjectives to describe yourself, and explain why you chose them. Ask your partner for a description.

SPEAKING ACTIVITY 13

Answer the following questionnaire by yourself. Then share your answers with a partner and give reasons for your choices. Get together with another pair of students. What do you have in common? What are your differences?

Questionnaire

1. Are you a day person or a night person?
2. Are you a city person or a country person?
3. Are you an outgoing person or a shy person?
4. Are you an adventurous person or a cautious person?
5. Are you confident or are you sometimes unsure of yourself?
6. Are you an optimist or a pessimist?
7. Are you independent or do you need to do things with others?
8. Are you persistent or do you give up easily?
9. Are you an easy-going person or are you a tense person?
10. Are you systematic and organized or are you disorganized?
11. Are you a hard-working person or are you a lazy person?
12. Are you energetic or are you a low energy person?

(continued . . .)

13. Are you impulsive or do you plan everything?

14. Are you a risk taker or are you careful?

15. Are you a serious person or are you lighthearted?

16. Are you a doer or are you an observer?

Communication Focus 6: Complimenting

English speakers often compliment each other. Compliments are a good way to let someone know that you like or admire them and to start a conversation. The most frequently used adjectives in compliments are *great*, *nice*, and *good*. Some other adjectives which we often use in compliments are *wonderful*, *terrific*, *fabulous*, *awesome*, *beautiful*, *amazing*, and *gorgeous*.

Structures/Expressions	Examples	Responses
I like/love . . .	I love your new bag. Where did you get it?	Thank you. I bought it when I was on holiday.
. . . looks great/fantastic/ awesome/terrific . . .	That shirt looks terrific on you.	Thank you. It's nice of you to say that. I got it for my birthday.
What a nice . . .	What a nice skirt!	Thanks. My aunt made it for me.
You did a good/excellent/ wonderful job . . .	You did a good job on this essay.	Thanks. It took a long time.
. . . is incredible	Your English is incredible!	Thank you for saying that.
. . . is beautiful/gorgeous/ fabulous	Is that your couch? It's really gorgeous!	Thanks. I'm glad you like it.

👥👥👥 SPEAKING ACTIVITY 14

Work in a group of three. Take turns giving each other compliments on articles of clothing, possessions, or actions. With each compliment, ask a question to get more information. Continue until each person in the group has given and responded to two compliments.

👥👥 SPEAKING ACTIVITY 15

Your instructor will borrow one item from each student in the class and put these into a bag or box and mix them up. Work with a partner. Take two items out and develop a role-play using complimenting. Present your role-play to the class. Listen for compliments and responses.

Communication Focus 7:
Handling Problems in Communication

Asking for Repetition or Clarification

1. Here are some expressions to use when you don't understand and you want the speaker to repeat or to rephrase the information in other words.

   Pardon me?

   I beg your pardon?

   Excuse me?

   Could you please repeat that?

   Pardon me, could you say that again, please?

   I'm sorry, I didn't get that.

   I'm sorry, I'm not following you.

   I am not sure I understand what you mean.

2. Here are some expressions to use if the speaker is speaking too quietly.

   Could you please speak up? I didn't catch that.

   I'm sorry, I didn't hear what you said.

3. Here is an expression to use if the speaker is speaking too quickly.

   Could you speak more slowly, please? I can't follow you.

4. Here are some phrases to use to check if the listener understands.

   Do you understand?

   Is that clear?

   Are you with me?

   Are you following me?

   Okay so far?

> **Speaking STRATEGY** 💬
>
> When you don't understand, don't feel nervous about asking the speaker to repeat as often as necessary.

👥 **SPEAKING ACTIVITY 16**

Work with a partner. Ask each other the following questions. Then join another pair of students and compare your answers.

1. How many languages are there in the world?
2. Which language do you think is the most difficult to learn? Why?
3. Do you think some languages are more beautiful than others?
4. Do you think a person can learn to speak a second language as well as a native speaker does?
5. Do you think a person's personality changes when they are speaking a second language?
6. What is the best age to start learning a second language?
7. What other languages would you like to learn? Why?
8. What is the most important language in the world?

LISTENING 2: LEARNING A NEW LANGUAGE—AN INTERVIEW

Before You Listen

Pre-listening Vocabulary

A. You will hear an interview on the audio CD that includes the following vocabulary. Work with a partner or by yourself to write the correct word next to its definition in the chart below.

experts	inhibited	to acquire	opportunities
extrovert	to participate	characteristics	strategy
to create	to monitor	outgoing	eager

Definitions	Vocabulary
1. qualities or features of someone or something	characteristics
2. to check something, to examine, to pay attention to something	
3. a person who is very friendly, talkative, and not reserved	
4. a plan or method; a way of doing something	
5. to make, to produce	
6. reserved, self-conscious; not relaxed or natural	
7. having a strong desire; keen, very interested in	
8. people with a lot of knowledge or skill in a particular area	
9. to take part, to get involved in	
10. to get, to receive; to develop or learn	
11. friendly, sociable; enjoying interactions with others	
12. chances; occasions	

B. Choose the correct vocabulary from the list above to fill in the blanks in these sentences. Use each word only once. Not all the words are used in the sentences. Please make changes to verbs or nouns when necessary.

1. Are you an _____extrovert_____ or an introvert?
2. At school students have many _____ to meet people.
3. Good language learners have certain _____ which help them _____ language more easily than others.
4. People who are shy or _____ can have a hard time learning a new language.
5. Good language learners use many _____ in learning a language.

6.　Good language learners are very ＿＿＿＿＿＿＿＿＿＿ to speak and ＿＿＿＿＿＿＿＿＿＿ in conversations whenever they can.

7.　If people are friendly and ＿＿＿＿＿＿＿＿＿＿, it's easier for them to meet new friends.

8.　My teacher says I need ＿＿＿＿＿＿＿＿＿＿ my grammar and try not to make mistakes.

9.　Psycholinguists are ＿＿＿＿＿＿＿＿＿＿ in how people learn languages.

10.　Let's ask our teacher ＿＿＿＿＿＿＿＿＿＿ some interesting games and activities for language learning.

👥 Pre-listening Activity

Work with a partner. You are going to hear an interview on the audio CD about learning a new language. Organize the following personality characteristics into the categories below.

Listening STRATEGY 👂

If you can preview the vocabulary and ideas that you are going to hear, it will be easier for you to understand the message.

eager to communicate

friendly and outgoing

shy

good guesser

tries everything to get the message across

embarrassed about making mistakes

extrovert

learns grammar rules

takes notes in class

systematic

organized

in charge of his or her learning

pretends not to understand

creates opportunities to use the language

nervous about speaking in a second language

upset about mistakes

memorizes vocabulary

afraid to make mistakes

Characteristics of a Good Language Learner	Characteristics of a Poor Language Learner	Characteristics You Are Not Sure About

Track 3

Listening for the Main Ideas

Listen to the interview once and answer the questions.

1. Who are the speakers and what is their relationship?
2. Where are they?
3. Why are they talking about this topic?

Listening Comprehension

 Track 4

Listen to the interview again. Write *T* if the statement is true or *F* if it is false.

1. Good language learners use many different strategies. _____
2. Good language learners look for opportunities to use the language. _____
3. Good language learners avoid talking to strangers. _____
4. Good language learners try only one method to get their message across. _____
5. Good language learners will stop paying attention if they don't understand. _____
6. Good language learners are good at guessing meaning. _____
7. Good language learners get upset if they don't understand all the words. _____
8. Good language learners don't have to work very hard at learning a second language. _____
9. Good language learners are upset about making mistakes. _____
10. Good language learners plan time for studying and practising. _____
11. Good language learners experiment with different methods of learning. _____
12. Good language learners take responsibility for their learning. _____
13. Good language learners are very emotional. _____

Personalizing

Discuss the following questions with your partner.

1. Which good-language-learner strategies do you use? Which ones do you want to acquire?
2. How can you acquire these new strategies?

VOCABULARY AND LANGUAGE CHUNKS

Write the number of each expression next to its meaning. After checking your answers, choose six expressions and write your own sentences.

Expressions	Meanings
1. to give up	__1__ to stop, to quit
2. to figure out	_____ I don't understand.
3. to hold on	_____ to put effort into, to keep trying
4. in charge of	_____ to be skilled, experienced at something
5. to put something into practice	_____ to be exactly right
6. to get a message across	_____ to make a quick judgment; to guess without having all the information
7. to hit the nail on the head	_____ to find the answer to, to discover, to solve
8. to be good at something	_____ to wait, to be patient
9. to work at	_____ in control of
10. I'm not following.	_____ to do something, to take action
11. to feel embarrassed	_____ to feel ashamed
12. to jump to conclusions	_____ to make someone understand a meaning

Listening STRATEGY

Evaluate your listening after each listening activity. Ask yourself how well you understood the main ideas. Don't be afraid to ask questions about points you did not understand very well.

PRONUNCIATION

Pronunciation Focus: Words with Predictable Stress Patterns

Pronouncing English words can be tricky. This is because words in English come from many sources, including German, French, Latin, and Greek. In English, when words have more than one syllable, not all the syllables receive the same stress. One of the syllables is usually pronounced longer, louder, and with higher pitch. Stressing a syllable means that we pronounce the vowel in that syllable louder, longer, and with higher pitch.

In some English words, however, there is very predictable word stress. In this chapter we are going to examine some words with predictable stress.

Track 5

PRONUNCIATION ACTIVITY 1

A. Listen to these words. Underline the stressed syllable in each word.

optimistic	conversation	attention	courageous
introduction	decision	curious	superstitious
energetic	opinion	opportunity	ambitious
characteristic	individual	individualistic	ability
communication	commercial	familiarity	originality
security	systematic	necessity	practical
enthusiastic	romantic	passion	comical
delicious	expression	comprehension	psychological
occupation	conclusion	grammatical	gorgeous

B. Check your answers with your partner. Together, figure out a rule for pronouncing these words by filling in the blanks in the rule below.

> When a word ends with one of these suffixes: *-ic, -_____,*
> *-_____, -_____, -ial, -sial, -cial, _____, -cious, -eous,* put
> the stress on the syllable directly _____
> the suffix.

Track 6

C. Listen again to the words and repeat them.

D. Working again with a partner, think of five other words with the same stress pattern. Share your answers with the class. Then, use as many of these words as you can to write a dialogue. Perform your dialogue for the class.

PRONUNCIATION ACTIVITY 2

 Track 7

A. Listen to these words and underline the stressed syllable.

table	pumpkin	apron	scissors
button	garden	pocket	folder
handle	picture	blanket	carpet
lettuce	barrel	pillow	purpose
illness	zipper	jacket	kitchen
cousin	turkey	ceiling	

B. Check your answers with your partner. Together, figure out a rule for pronouncing these words by filling in the blanks in the rule below.

> In English _____ with _____
> syllables, the stress falls on the _____ syllable
> in more than 90 percent of the cases.

Track 8

C. Listen again to the words and repeat them.

PRONUNCIATION ACTIVITY 3

A. Listen to these words and underline the stressed syllable.

 **Track 9**

airport	armchair	toenail	backpack
driveway	ashtray	raincoat	sunglasses
greenhouse	bookstore	bluebird	blackbird
blackboard	classroom	doorbell	eyebrow
haircut	headache	bookcase	

B. Check your answers with your partner. Together, figure out a rule for pronouncing these words by filling in the blanks in the rule below.

In compound nouns, the major stress falls on the _____ syllable of the compound noun.

C. Listen again to the words and repeat them.

 **Track 10**

PRONUNCIATION ACTIVITY 4

A. Listen to these words and underline the stressed syllable.

 Track 11

escape	forget	attract	contain
admire	request	receive	decide
suggest	improve	conclude	improve
survive	surprise	respect	admit
offend	replace	protect	announce
forgive	arrest	repeat	

B. Check your answers with your partner. Together, figure out a rule for pronouncing these words by filling in the blanks in the rule below.

In English _____ with _____ syllables, the stress falls on the _____ syllable about 60 percent of the time.

C. Listen again to the words and repeat them.

 **Track 12**

PRONUNCIATION ACTIVITY 5

A. Listen carefully. You will hear a word followed by an example sentence with that word. After listening to each example, underline the stressed syllable in the word.

 **Track 13**

record: He kept a record.

record: He recorded his voice.

conduct: They conducted themselves very well.

conduct: Their conduct was very good.

produce: This country produces agricultural products.

produce: They sell the extra produce to other countries.

project: They worked hard on the project.

project: The bank projected higher profits for the coming year.

progress: They made great progress in learning English.

progress: He progressed to the final stage.

suspect: She suspected him of committing the crime.

suspect: The police want to question the suspect.

B. Check your answers with your partner. Together, figure out a rule for pronouncing these words by filling in the blanks in the rule below.

If the word is a _____, the stress falls

on the _____ syllable. If the word

is a _____, the stress falls on the

_____ syllable.

 Track 14   **C.** Listen again and repeat the words and sentences after the speaker.

 Track 15   **PRONUNCIATION ACTIVITY 6**

Listen to the words in each of the lists. For each list, decide which word does not belong. Circle it.

Clue: Pay attention to the stressed syllable.

1.	2.	3.	4.	5.
ice cream	complain	backache	combine	mysterious
syrup	release	head band	destroy	millionaire
pepper	resume	today	delight	permission
winter	elect	ear ache	capture	anxiety
travel	summer	bracelet	devote	delicious
July	resign	earring	disturb	ambition

PRONUNCIATION ACTIVITY 7

A. In the chart on the next page, put the words in the first column into the correct category, according to the stress patterns.

	[ta**ta**ta] example: oc**ca**sion	[**ta**tata] example: **com**pliment	[ta**ta**] example: to**day**	[**ta**ta] example: **heart**ache
tomorrow				
beautiful				
September				
different				
October				
friendliness				
fantastic				
mistake				
happiness				
sorrow				
confident				
homework				
breakdown				
shoelace				
awesome				
jealous				
believe				
wristwatch				
terrific				
selfish				
honest				
restless				
practical				
November				
sincere				
sorry				
excellent				
wonderful				
competent				
pessimist				
cautious				
optimist				
bother				
imagine				

B. Listen to the words and check your answers.  **Track 16**

C. With two partners, use as many of the words as possible to make up dialogues.

COMMUNICATING IN THE REAL WORLD

Use your English to talk to people outside your classroom. On your own or with a partner, talk to five people outside your class. Make up your own questions based on the topics in this chapter or ask the questions below and record the information.

Make a short report to the class about what you learned.

Here is one way to introduce your assignment.

> Could I ask you some questions? I am doing an assignment for my English class.

1. How many languages do you speak?
2. How did you learn your new language?
3. What language would you like to learn?
4. What's the best way to learn a language? Why?
5. What is the most important language in the world?

SELF-EVALUATION

Think about your work in this chapter. For each row in the chart sections **Grammar and Language Functions**, **Learning Strategies**, and **Pronunciation**, give yourself a score based on the rating scale below and write a comment in the Notes section.

Show the chart to your teacher. Talk about what you need to do to make your English better.

Rating Scale

1	2	3	4	5

Needs improvement. ⟵————————————⟶ *Great!*

	Score	Notes
Grammar and Language Functions		
introducing myself and others		
talking about facts and habits using the simple present tense		
using conversation openers		
extending and responding to invitations		
expressing future plans using the present progressive tense		
describing personal characteristics using adjectives		
complimenting people and responding to compliments		
handling problems in communication		
Pronunciation		
pronouncing words with predictable stress patterns		
Learning Strategies		
Speaking		
when introducing people, giving some interesting information about them or pointing out something they have in common so that a conversation can begin		
asking the speaker to repeat as often as necessary when I don't understand		
Listening		
thinking about what I am going to hear, and trying to predict what people will say, to help improve my comprehension		
previewing the vocabulary and ideas that I am going to hear, to make it easier for me to understand the listening		
evaluating my listening comprehension after each listening activity and asking questions about points that I did not understand very well		

Vocabulary and Language Chunks
Look at this list of new vocabulary and language chunks you learned in this chapter. Give yourself a score based on the rating scale and write a comment.

to make friends	all set	to get to
by the way	to stay up	in time
to take a lot of time	to get up	to give someone a call
in no time	to get on	to wait for
to have people over	to give someone a shout	to give up
tons of	to hold on	to figure out
to get a message across	to be good at	I'm not following
to hit the nail on the head	to work at	to jump to conclusions
to be into	to look forward to	no big deal
to drop by	in charge	put something into practice
to feel embarrassed		

	Score	Notes
understanding new vocabulary and language chunks		
using new words and phrases correctly		

Write eight sentences and use new vocabulary you learned in this chapter.

1. _____

2. _____

3. _____

4. _____

5. _____

6. _____

7. _____

8. _____

My plan for practising is _____

_____

_____

_____

CHAPTER 2

Telling It as It Was

Experiences and Achievements

Talking about past experiences, narrating

Encouraging conversation

Describing past habits

Explaining

Talking about similarities and differences

Paraphrasing

THINKING AND TALKING

Who are these people? What did they do in their lives?

A. Work with a partner. Put the famous people in the following list into the categories below in the chart. Choose five people and explain why they are famous. What did they do?

John Lennon	Mao Tse Tung	Alexander Graham Bell
Cleopatra	Pablo Picasso	Ernest Hemingway
George Washington	Bill Gates	Michael Jackson
Charles Dickens	Albert Einstein	Céline Dion
Leonardo da Vinci	Avril Lavigne	William Shakespeare
Barack Obama	Thomas Edison	Elvis Presley
Nelson Mandela	Christopher Columbus	Farley Mowat

Artists and Writers	Singers and Musicians	Politicians and Rulers	Inventors and Discoverers

B. Join another pair of students and compare your answers.

C. What are some questions you would like to ask five of these people? Report the most interesting questions to the class.

LISTENING 1: FARLEY MOWAT, A FAMOUS CANADIAN—A NEWS REPORT

Before You Listen

Pre-listening Vocabulary

A. You will hear a report on the audio CD that includes the following vocabulary. Work with a partner or by yourself to write the correct word next to its definition in the chart below.

battle	brutality	species	morality	underdog
to encounter	image	appalled	to extirpate	grandeur
company	inspiration	invasion	realization	slaughter
outrage	accuracy	vicious	predator	to cull
feisty	fascinating	fuel	plight	prairies
consequence				

Definitions	Vocabulary
1. a fight or conflict	battle
2. something used to produce energy or power	
3. dangerous, difficult, or unfortunate situation	
4. very interesting	
5. very strong feeling of anger, shock, and disapproval	
6. correctness; preciseness	
7. cruel, cold-blooded; violent	
8. an animal that kills and eats others	
9. something that stimulates the mind or emotions	
10. a group of people; being together with people	
11. the act of an enemy entering another country	
12. the act of understanding or realizing	
13. to kill off; to destroy completely	
14. shocked, disgusted, very angry	
15. picture	
16. to meet; to find	
17. great physical violence and cruelty	
18. beliefs about what is right and what is wrong, and what is good and what is bad	
19. a group of plants or animals that are similar in many ways	
20. someone that people think will lose; someone who has no chance of winning a contest	

continued on next page

Definitions	Vocabulary
21. grandness, awesomeness	
22. large open areas of grassland, as in the provinces of Manitoba and Saskatchewan in Canada	
23. violent killing	
24. to do a selective killing of wild animals	
25. result or effect of something	
26. not afraid to fight or argue; lively, spunky	

B. Choose the correct vocabulary from the list above to fill in the blanks in these sentences. Use each word only once. Not all the words are used in the sentences. Please make changes to verbs or nouns when necessary.

1. Many people died in the _____*battle*_____ between the two countries.

2. She is always ready to fight for her opinions. She's very _____.

3. The people had a feeling of _____ when they learned about the terrible conditions in the schools.

4. The beauty of nature is an _____ to many artists and writers.

5. In the past, people thought that wolves were _____ _____ because they sometimes killed cattle.

6. Ranchers and farmers _____ many wolves because they feared them.

7. Mowat always fought for the _____, the one who had little chance of succeeding.

8. He reported with great _____. His reports were always correct.

9. They _____ many _____ of wild animals on their journeys in Africa.

10. People wanted to reduce the number of wolves. They asked the government _____ the wolf population.

👥 Pre-listening Activity

Read about Farley Mowat's achievements below. You can also find out more information by going to websites about him.

With a partner make a list of what you know about Farley Mowat and what you would like to learn about him.

Some Highlights of Farley Mowat's Achievements

Farley Mowat, author, environmentalist, and activist, was born on 12 May 1921 in Belleville, Ontario. Mowat is one of Canada's most

famous authors. His books are available in 52 languages and they have sold more than 17 million copies around the world. Sometimes people attacked his work because they said he exaggerated, but he defended himself by saying he "never lets facts get in the way of the truth." Most readers praised him. He usually wrote about creatures living in the natural world—both animal and human. His first book, *People of the Deer,* was about a tribe in Northern Canada whose living conditions outraged Mowat. His most famous book, *Never Cry Wolf* (1963), helped to change the negative reputation of wolves as vicious killers, and helped to stop the killing of wolves in Russia. *Never Cry Wolf* was made into a movie in 1983.

Adapted from the website of *The Canadian Encyclopedia.*

What We Know about Farley Mowat	What We Would Like to Learn about Farley Mowat

Listening for the Main Ideas

Listen to the news report about Farley Mowat and then answer the questions.

 Track 17

1. What important things did Farley Mowat do?
2. How do the speakers feel about Farley Mowat?
3. What is the reason for this news report?

Listening Comprehension

Listen to the report again as many times as necessary. As you listen, number the events in the order in which they are mentioned.

 Track 18

_____ Farley Mowat joined the Allied invasion of Sicily during the Second World War.

_____ Farley Mowat was born in Ontario.

_____ Mowat's book *People of the Deer* started a debate about Canada's policies in the Arctic.

__1__ Farley Mowat was a fierce defender of the natural world.

_____ Farley Mowat grew up in Saskatchewan.

_____ Early family pets inspired his books for children.

_____ Farley Mowat experienced the worst of the brutality of human against human.

_____ *Never Cry Wolf* changed the image of the wolf and stopped wolf culls in Russia.

_____ Farley Mowat's motto was "Never let the facts get in the way of the truth."

_____ Farley Mowat took aim at the seal hunt.

_____ Some people criticized Farley Mowat's factual accuracy.

Personalizing

Work in a group of four. Discuss these questions and report to the class.

1. What did you learn about Farley Mowat and Canada?
2. What surprised you about Farley Mowat?
3. How do you think Canadians can honour Farley Mowat?

VOCABULARY AND LANGUAGE CHUNKS

Write the number of each expression next to its meaning. After checking your answers, choose six expressions and write your own sentences.

Expressions	Meanings
1. to grow up	__1__ to change from being a child to an adult
2. to leave all that behind	_____ the people who have power
3. natural world	_____ to kill someone or to take revenge on someone
4. to fight for the underdog	_____ to want to do something very much and not let anything stop you
5. to be appalled	_____ to block, stop, prevent something from happening
6. to die off	_____ to change the way people see something
7. to get to know	_____ to speak up for the one with the disadvantage
8. to bring something alive	_____ nature and life on earth, not changed by humans
9. to change the image of	_____ to go on, to leave, to depart
10. to get in the way of	_____ to make something live, be alive, vivid
11. to be determined	_____ to become acquainted with, familiar with
12. the powers that be	_____ to stop living [used when all the members of a group die]
13. to get someone	_____ to be shocked, very angry, disgusted

SPEAKING 1

Communication Focus 1:
Talking about Past Experiences, Narrating

Structures/Expressions	Examples
Once when I . . .	Once when I was walking home late in the evening, I saw a ghost.
What happened was . . .	What happened was that one of my neighbours was playing a trick on some friends because it was Halloween.
I remember when . . .	I remember when I first saw him in his costume, I screamed.
I'll never forget the time . . .	I'll never forget the time that I was so scared I couldn't move.

Listening STRATEGY

Listen for signals that tell you the order in which things happened. Listening for words like *first*, *then*, *after that*, and *finally* will help you to understand the sequence of events or the times when actions happened in the past.

Questions/Conversation Stimulators

Here are some sentence starters and questions we can ask when talking about past events.

What happened when . . .

Tell me about the time . . .

What did you do when . . .

Tell me about what happened next.

What happened after that?

Sequence Markers/Time Signals

When we retell past events in chronological order (the order in which they happened), we often use sequence markers or signals such as the following to make the time of the events clear.

first	first of all	to begin with		
then	next	after that	at that time	at that point
finally	in the end			

SPEAKING ACTIVITY 1

Work with a partner. Tell your partner about an interesting movie or TV program that you saw recently. Use sequence markers or signals to tell the story. Your partner will report to the class.

Grammar Note: The Simple Past Tense

When we talk about a completed action in the past, we use the simple past tense. Most verbs take the regular past tense ending *-ed*, but some of the verbs we use most often are irregular.

Affirmative	Negative	Interrogative
Jane lost her passport last year.	She didn't lose her purse.	Did she lose anything else?
Ricardo watched a movie last night.	He didn't watch the news.	Did he watch the football game too?
Larry was at work yesterday.	He wasn't at home.	Was Maria at work too?

 SPEAKING ACTIVITY 2

Walk around the room and ask questions to find people who did each of the things in the chart below. When you find someone who did one of the actions ask them to write their name in the box. Try to get as many names as possible.

Examples:

Did you forget something recently?

Did you take public transit today?

drank coffee recently:	lost something recently:	saw an English movie recently:	was angry about something recently:
read an English story recently:	took public transit today:	got good marks on a test recently:	met some new friends recently:
moved to a new place recently:	made a mistake recently:	forgot something recently:	had a great weekend:
went to the library:	bought something recently:	visited a friend recently:	heard some English songs recently:
studied for a test recently:	took a trip recently:	cooked something recently:	got a present recently:

Grammar Note: Past Progressive Tense

When we talk about an action that was in progress at a specific point in the past we use the past progressive tense. Look at the examples in the chart on the next page. How do we form this tense?

Affirmative	Negative	Interrogative
Jane **was** travel**ling** in China last May.	She **wasn't** travelling alone.	**Was** she travel**ling** on a visitor's visa?
They **were** us**ing** computers at 10:30 this morning.	They **weren't** using the camera equipment.	**Were** they us**ing** the Internet?

SPEAKING ACTIVITY 3

Work with a partner and tell each other a folk tale or a fairy tale (for example, "Cinderella," "The Three Pigs," "The Three Monks," "The Butterfly Lovers") from your country. Use sequence markers such as *first, next, then,* and *after that.*

SPEAKING ACTIVITY 4

Work in a group of three. Individually, choose one of the topics below to talk about. Use time expressions and sequence markers such as *first, next, then,* and *after that.* Other students will ask questions as you tell your story. When everyone has finished, report about the most unusual information you found out.

Speaking STRATEGY

Use signals such as *then, after that,* and *finally* to make it easier for listeners to understand when events happened.

Topics

The first time I fell in love	My greatest achievement so far
My first trip	My first day in this country/city
The most important event in my life so far	A happy day in my life

Communication Focus 2: Encouraging Conversation

One way to keep a conversation going is to ask open-ended questions. These are different from *Yes/No* questions (closed questions). A *Yes/No* question only requires "yes" or "no" as an answer and the conversation may end. An open-ended question begins with a question word and encourages conversation because the other person will give more information, which can lead to more questions and information.

Yes/No Questions (Closed Questions)

> Are you a student?
>
> Did you drive to work?
>
> Do you like to travel?

Questions that begin with a question word but require very specific answers are also closed questions.

> Where are you from?
>
> What language do you speak?

Open-Ended Questions

Why are you studying at this school?

How did you feel when you first came here?

What do you want to do in your life?

👥 SPEAKING ACTIVITY 5

Work with a partner. Each of you will choose a topic of your own from the list below. One partner makes a statement about his or her topic. The other partner will ask as many open-ended questions as possible for two minutes. The first partner will answer the questions. Then reverse roles. When you finish, change partners and start again. Report about some interesting information that you learned.

Topics

My dream job

The last time I went to a restaurant/party/movie

A good experience

The strangest thing I have ever seen

What I want to do in my life

My first day here

My favourite pastime

Communication Focus 3: Describing Past Habits

We use *used to* + the base form of the verb to talk about habitual actions or states in the past which are no longer true. We also use *would* to talk about habitual actions in the past, but not about states.

Examples:

I *used to live* in a small town and I *would ride* my bicycle everywhere.

(I don't live in a small town and ride my bicycle everywhere anymore.)

I *didn't use to speak* English very well and I *would make* many mistakes.

(I speak English well and don't make many mistakes now.)

Did Andrea *use to* smoke?

(She doesn't smoke now.)

Ellen and Sherry *didn't use to* live downtown.

(They live downtown now.)

👥 SPEAKING ACTIVITY 6

Work in a group of three. Find out the following information from each person in your group and then choose someone to report some interesting facts to the class. Remember to ask open-ended questions to keep your conversations going.

Questions	Partner 1	Partner 2
What did you use to look like as a teenager?		
Where did you use to live?		
What did you use to do in your free time?		
What problems did you use to have?		
What used to make you happy at that time?		
What used to be important to you when you were younger?		
Describe the friends you used to have then.		
What did you use to dream of doing?		
What didn't you use to do that you do now?		

SPEAKING ACTIVITY 7

A. Work with a partner. Read this article about women. Replace the verbs with *used to* or *would*.

> Life has changed a great deal for women in North America in the past 100 years. In the early 1900s, daily life *was* completely different for women. Women *didn't have* the right to vote. Most women *were* housewives and homemakers. Most women *stayed* home and *took* care of children. Women *were* responsible for all the housework. Women *washed* clothes by hand and they *cooked* meals from scratch. There *was* discrimination against women in many professions. Most women *didn't get* very much education. Women didn't *compete* in the Olympics. There *were* no women pilots or sports figures. Thank goodness things have changed. Women are much better off today and they don't want life to be the way it *was* 100 years ago.

B. Now discuss some differences between you and your parents or grandparents. Use *used to* or *would*. You can use pictures of yourself and your parents from the past, if you want.

Communication Focus 4: Explaining

When we give explanations, we often talk about the causes or the results of an event. We use transition words or logical connectors to make the relationships between the ideas clear.

Stating Reasons

We can state reasons by using logical connectors such as *because, because of, since,* and *due to*.
Examples:

>My favourite singer is Avril Lavigne *because* (*since*) she has a great voice.

>Avril Lavigne is my favourite singer *because of* (*due to*) her great voice.

Stating Results

We can use logical connectors such as *so, therefore,* and *as a result* to state results.
Examples:

>Beyoncé is a great performer so she is very popular.

>Beyoncé is a wonderful singer; therefore, she is very popular.

>Beyoncé is a fantastic performer, and as a result, she is very popular.

SPEAKING ACTIVITY 8

A. Work with a partner. Choose a famous person and a famous place.

Famous person: _____ Famous place: _____

List as many reasons as you can for their fame. Use different logical connectors for stating reasons.

B. Then make a list of as many results of their fame as you can. Use logical connectors for stating results. The pair with the longest and the most interesting lists is the winner.

SPEAKING ACTIVITY 9

Work in a small group. Discuss the reasons for and results of the events in the chart below. Present your ideas to the class.

Events	Reasons	Results
The dinosaurs disappeared from the earth.		
The ice age ended.		
The earth is getting warmer.		
Humans landed on and explored the moon.		
Bill Gates developed an operating system for computers.		
The US government developed the Internet in the latter part of the twentieth century.		
Social networking websites are extremely popular.		

LISTENING 2: THE MOST VISITED PLACES IN THE WORLD—A REPORT

Before You Listen

ᏪᏪ Pre-listening Activity

Where are these places? What other famous tourist attractions do you know?

Work in a small group. Look at the following list of countries. Decide which five are the most-visited countries in the world.

Japan   Australia   United States   Thailand
Turkey   Spain   Italy   France
China   Mexico   Egypt   Greece

1. _____
2. _____
3. _____
4. _____
5. _____

ᏪᏪ Pre-listening Vocabulary

A. You will hear a report on the audio CD that includes the following vocabulary. Work with a partner or by yourself to write the correct word next to its definition in the chart below.

attraction   incredible   source   tourist
masters   to be impressed palace   doubt
memories   souvenir   spot   resort
skyscrapers   to roam   to marvel   ancient
cruise   monument

Definitions	Vocabulary
1. a pleasure trip by boat	cruise
2. beyond belief, unbelievable; amazing	
3. to be full of wonder, amazement	
4. uncertainty; questioning	
5. to walk around; to wander around	
6. to be excited about and to admire what you see	
7. famous or historical building, statue, or structure	
8. very old, from the distant past	
9. very tall buildings	
10. thing or place that attracts tourists	
11. a vacation place where people stay	
12. recollections; what people remember	
13. experts	
14. a person who travels to visit new places	
15. very big, beautiful house where a king or queen or other ruler lives	
16. something tourists buy in foreign places to help them remember their trip	
17. the place where something (such as information) comes from	
18. place	

B. Choose the correct vocabulary from the list above to fill in the blanks in these sentences. Use each word only once. Not all the words are used in the sentences. Please make changes to verbs or nouns when necessary.

1. Janice and her family took a _____cruise_____ on the Amazon River.

2. What's the difference between a traveller and a _____?

3. When I visited Spain I stayed at a beautiful _____ on the beach.

4. She visited the royal _____ in Tokyo and she thought it was _____.

5. We bought _____ when we visited the White House and other famous _____ in Washington.

6. I have no _____ that all the tourists who go to China want to visit its most famous _____, the Great Wall.

7. If you go to Shanghai you will be very _____ by all the modern _____ beside the river.

8. When we were in France we _____ at all the delicious food and pastries. The French are _____ at cooking and baking.

9. I'll never forget my trip to Japan. I have some wonderful _____ of it.

10. Do you know a good _____ to have lunch downtown?

Listening for the Main Ideas

Listen to the report, and then answer the questions.

 Track 19

1. What kind of program is this?
2. What is the purpose of the program?
3. What are the main things the speaker talks about?

Listening Comprehension

Listen as many times as necessary and answer the questions.

 Track 20

1. What was the most-visited country in the world and how many tourists went there? What two things did people do there?
2. What was the second-most-visited country and how many tourists went there? What did people do there?
3. What was the third-most-visited country? How many tourists did it receive?
4. What was the fourth-most-visited country? How many visitors did it receive? What did people do there?
5. What was the fifth-most-visited country? How many visitors did it receive?

Listening STRATEGY

Listening for numbers and for signal words which tell the order of something (for example, *first*, *second*, and *third*) will help you understand details.

Personalizing

Discuss the following with a partner.

1. Have you visited any of these places?
2. Which places would you like to visit? Explain why.
3. Why do so many people travel these days?

VOCABULARY AND LANGUAGE CHUNKS

Write the number of each expression next to its meaning. After checking your answers, choose six expressions and write your own sentences.

Expressions

1. to have no doubt
2. to go sightseeing
3. to take home memories
4. to go dancing
5. to take a cruise
6. well worth visiting
7. to get going
8. never a better time
9. tourist attraction
10. to be home to
11. to take photographs
12. to go swimming
13. up to date
14. second spot

Meanings

_____ to visit special sights and places

_____ to remember experiences when one returns home

_____ to spend time dancing

_____ to travel by boat

_____ to be the place where something is located

_____ the best time is now, no time is better

_____ newest, most recent

_____ a place tourists visit

_____ to spend time swimming

__1__ to be sure

_____ second place

_____ to start to do something

_____ worth the time and money to visit

_____ to take pictures

SPEAKING 2

Communication Focus 5: Talking about Similarities and Differences

Structures/Expressions	Examples
similar to . . .	Travelling in North America is similar to travelling in Europe.
the same as . . .	Travelling in the US is the same as travelling in Canada.
as . . . as . . .	Trains are as comfortable as planes.
different from . . .	Travelling by bus is different from travelling by car.

Grammar Note: Comparative and Superlative Forms

We can use comparative and superlative forms of adjectives and adverbs to talk about similarities and differences.

SHORT (ONE-SYLLABLE) ADJECTIVES

Comparative Forms

We make the comparative forms of short (one-syllable) adjectives and adverbs by adding –*er* to the adjective or adverb.
Examples:

> Canada is bigger than France.
>
> Mexicans are happier than Canadians.

Superlative Forms

We make the superlative forms of short adjectives and adverbs by adding –*est* to the adjective or adverb.

When the adjective or adverb ends in –*y*, replace the *y* with *i* and add –*er* or –*est*.
Examples:

> Russia is the biggest country in the world.
>
> I think Mexicans are the happiest people in North America.
>
> Who do you think are the friendliest people in the world?

Irregular Forms

The comparative and superlative forms of the irregular adjectives *good* and *bad* are:

good, better, the best   bad, worse, the worst
Examples:

> Are you a *good* traveller? Yes, but my sister is *better*. She's *the best* traveller in the family.
>
> Is the weather in London *bad* in winter? Yes, it's *worse* than the weather in Rome. London has *the worst* weather in Europe.

ADJECTIVES AND ADVERBS OF TWO OR MORE SYLLABLES

With adjectives and adverbs of two or more syllables, we use *more/less . . . than* for comparative forms and *the most/the least . . .* for superlative forms.

Comparative Forms

> I think Paris is more beautiful than Los Angeles.
>
> New York is more exciting than Chicago.

Superlative Forms

> Paris is the most beautiful city in the world.
>
> New York is the most exciting city in North America.

COMPARATIVE AND SUPERLATIVE WITH NOUNS

We can also use *more/less, less/fewer,* and *the least/the fewest/the most* with nouns.
Examples:

> Travelling is more fun than staying at home.
>
> Staying home costs less money than travelling.

France had the most tourists in 2014.

We had the fewest problems travelling in the US.

North Americans have the least time to travel.

ii SPEAKING ACTIVITY 10

Work with a partner, and interview him or her. Report the most interesting answers to the class.

Questions	Partner's Responses
1. Describe the best trip you took. Where did you go? How did you go? Who did you go with?	
2. What was the worst trip you took?	
3. What do you like doing the most on vacation?	
4. What countries have you visited? Compare two of them.	
5. What cities have you visited? Compare two of them.	
6. What is your favourite city or country to visit? Why?	
7. What is most important to you when you are travelling in a new city?	
8. What is the most convenient thing to have on a trip?	
9. What is the most beautiful place you have visited?	
10. What is the most interesting place you have visited?	
11. Compare travelling by yourself to travelling with a group.	
12. What's your favourite way to travel: bus, train, car, boat, bicycle, or backpacking? Explain why.	
13. What do you like the least about travelling?	

iii SPEAKING ACTIVITY 11

Work in a group. Make as many comparisons as you can about the following topics. The teacher will give you a certain period of time. At the end of this time, the group with the most comparisons wins!

1. Staying home/travelling

2. Travelling in this country/travelling in foreign countries

3. Camping/staying in hotels

4. Plane travel/train travel

5. Taking a cruise/taking a driving holiday
6. Hiking/cycling
7. A vacation in the country/a city vacation
8. Visiting museums and monuments/visiting the countryside
9. Visiting ancient places/visiting modern cities and areas
10. Vacationing at a beach/vacationing in the mountains

🕵 SPEAKING ACTIVITY 12

Work with a partner. Make as many comparisons as you can about the following topics.

1. tourists/travellers
2. man-made tourist attractions/natural sites that people visit
3. men/women
4. teenagers/adults
5. teachers/students

Speaking STRATEGY 💬

Control your nervousness and your emotions when you are speaking. Don't be afraid to ask for help from others when you have problems expressing your ideas.

Communication Focus 6: Paraphrasing

When we paraphrase we explain the same idea in different and usually simpler words.

Original Sentences	Paraphrases
He intended to purchase an exquisite gift for his beloved.	He planned to buy a nice present for his sweetheart.
Travel brings out the best and the worst traits in human beings.	When they travel, people can do very good and very bad things.

🕵 SPEAKING ACTIVITY 13

Work with a partner to paraphrase the following proverbs.

Proverbs	Paraphrases
You can't judge a book by its cover.	
All that glitters is not gold.	
A stitch in time saves nine.	
The early bird catches the worm.	
Heaven helps those who help themselves.	
Rome was not built in a day.	
When in Rome, do as the Romans do.	
Birds of a feather flock together.	
You can lead a horse to water but you can't make it drink.	

Can you think of other proverbs? If so, add them to the list and paraphrase them.

SPEAKING ACTIVITY 14

Look at the list of words below. Check off the ones you know. Walk around the room and ask other people to explain the words you don't know until you understand all the words. Try to paraphrase when giving explanations.

adventure	atmosphere	accommodation	leisurely
boulevard	vehicle	night life	byways
glacier	unique	wildlife	scenery
disembark	surrounding	remote	

 **SPEAKING ACTIVITY 15**

Work in a group.

Good news! You and your group have just won an all-expenses-paid trip to one of the following places. You need to agree on the place that you will visit. Discuss the advantages and disadvantages of the trip, and the reasons for your choice. Present your choice and your reason for it to the rest of the class.

Speaking STRATEGY 💬

When you don't know or can't think of a word, look for different ways to express the idea. Use synonyms or paraphrase.

Adventure 1

Patagonia, Glacier Adventure: You start your adventure in Buenos Aires, the capital of Argentina. Spend six nights in a five-star hotel in this European-style city with wide boulevards and an exciting night life. Then take a cruise to Patagonia to see the glaciers. Explore Punta Arenas—watch seals and penguins. See and hear blocks of ice breaking free and crashing into the sea. Visit Ushuaia, the world's most southern city. Finally, disembark in Santiago, a modern city surrounded by snowy mountains before you fly back to Buenos Aires. What's included? Accommodation, cruise, hotels, most meals, transfers—14 days.

Adventure 2

India and the Taj Mahal: There is no better way to see village life in Northern India than by cycling and camel riding. Start off by spending two days in Delhi. Then, go by train to northern India. We combine cycling and camel riding with visits to famous palaces and forts. We start off in the desert, and our camel caravan takes us to remote villages and forts. We visit the city of Jodhpur and the Pink City of Jaipur before starting our cycle ride. If you haven't cycled since your school days, don't worry. The roads are flat, the days are relaxed, and we have a backup van for your convenience. We finish by watching the sun rise at the Taj Mahal. Afterward, there will be train transportation back to Delhi. What's included? Accommodation in good hotels, all meals, camels, bicycles, all transfers, and train travel—15 days.

Adventure 3

Africa Adventure: Imagine seeing the plains of Tanzania from the top of Africa's highest mountain—Mount Kilimanjaro. East Africa's amazing parks and its highest mountain are included in this unique vacation. You get the incredible chance to experience hiking to the top of Mt Kilimanjaro and then through Masai country, looking for wildlife. Combining the walks with wild animal viewing is a truly East African experience. What's included? All meals, all transfers, all national park and conservation fees, one night of four-star hotel accommodation in Nairobi, four nights' accommodation at a three-star hotel, safari-style tents, and all group camping and catering equipment, including a supply van—16 days.

Adventure 4

Cycling Vietnam: Riding a mountain bike along the highways and byways of Vietnam is one of the most rewarding ways to experience this country. Travelling the same way as the local people lets you interact with the many Vietnamese people you will meet on this adventure. We explore mountains, palm-lined beaches, and country roads. Along our route you will be in contact with the real Vietnam—an experience you will never forget. What's included? English-speaking tour leader, group medical kit, all hotel accommodations, all meals, airport transfers, all group transport including the train from Hanoi to Hue in an air-conditioned soft-sleeper carriage, domestic flight to Ho Chi Minh City, use of a mountain bicycle, and sightseeing excursions—15 days.

ﬁﬁﬁ SPEAKING ACTIVITY 16

Work in a group. Research and plan the trip of a lifetime—the most exciting and memorable trip a person can take. Make a poster or PowerPoint presentation about your trip. Give descriptions of the activities and places you will visit. Make a presentation about your trip to the class. The class will vote for the best trip and explain why they chose it.

PRONUNCIATION

Pronunciation Focus: Regular Past Tense Endings

The pronunciation of the regular past tense ending *-ed* differs depending on the verb.

In some verbs the past tense ending is pronounced / d /: for example, *played*, *called*, and *tried*.

In some verbs the ending is pronounced / t /: for example, *kicked*, *washed*, and *danced*.

In some verbs the ending is pronounced / əd /: for example, *wanted*, *needed*, and *painted*.

PRONUNCIATION ACTIVITY 1

Track 21

A. Listen to these verbs. Write the correct pronunciation of the past tense as / t /, / d /, or / əd /.

cooked _____	prayed _____	punished _____
looked _____	shopped _____	wanted _____
washed _____	hoped _____	attended _____
finished _____	lived _____	decided _____
competed _____	enjoyed _____	pressured _____
played _____	voted _____	asked _____
changed _____	killed _____	planned _____
waited _____	discriminated _____	refused _____
stayed _____	promised _____	

Track 22

B. Listen again and repeat each verb after you hear it.

PRONUNCIATION ACTIVITY 2

Track 23

A. Listen to these verbs. Write the pronunciation of the past tense ending.

needed _____	invited _____
wanted _____	added _____
started _____	visited _____
ended _____	decided _____

B. Work with a partner and figure out the rule for the pronunciation of the past tense of these verbs by filling in the blanks below.

When the verb stem ends in _____ or

_____, pronounce the past tense ending as

_____.

Track 24

C. Listen again and repeat each verb after you hear it.

PRONUNCIATION ACTIVITY 3

Track 25

A. Listen to these verbs. Write the pronunciation of the past tense ending.

washed _____	bumped _____	helped _____	tripped _____
laughed _____	watched _____	coughed _____	punched _____
fished _____	finished _____	danced _____	dressed _____
liked _____	stuffed _____	ranked _____	
talked _____	stopped _____	hiked _____	

B. Work with a partner and figure out the rule for the pronunciation of the past tense of these verbs by filling in the blanks below.

When the verb stem ends in a _____ sound,

pronounce the past tense ending as _____.

C. Listen again, and repeat each verb after you hear it.   Track 26

PRONUNCIATION ACTIVITY 4

A. Listen to these verbs. Write the pronunciation of the past tense ending.   Track 27

lived _____   rained _____   viewed _____   cried _____

closed _____   roamed _____   showed _____   starred _____

wandered _____   called _____   smiled _____   cycled _____

tried _____   played _____   answered _____

B. Work with a partner and figure out the rule for the pronunciation of the past tense of these verbs by filling in the blanks below.

When the verb stem ends in a _____ sound,

pronounce the past tense ending as _____.

C. Listen again, and repeat each verb after you hear it.   Track 28

PRONUNCIATION ACTIVITY 5

A. Say these sentences to a partner.

1. She turned down the marriage proposal.
2. They travelled on a cruise ship.
3. Mary Anne started off skiing on the lowest hills.
4. Man landed on the moon ages ago.
5. Ali stayed at home last summer.
6. The students biked along the paths in the park.
7. We shopped in the best stores.
8. Tom climbed up to the top of the mountain.
9. They called off their travel plans.
10. Anna looked up the prices of the flights.

B. Listen to the sentences. Were your sentences correct?   Track 29

PRONUNCIATION ACTIVITY 6

Work in a small group. Tell each other three things that you did in the past in your free time using the following list of verbs. Two of the statements you make should be true and one should be false. People can guess which one is false. The person who guesses correctly takes the next turn.

visit	shop	dance	invite	walk
sail	enjoy	try	amuse	snorkel
act	ski	contact	play	watch
decide	hike	stay	paint	discover
travel	call up	bike	view	

PRONUNCIATION ACTIVITY 7

Work in a group of four. Make up a story using the following verbs in the past tense. The first person will choose a verb and make a statement. The second person chooses another verb and makes a statement that follows the first sentence. Continue until you have used at least 10 sentences with 10 verbs. The group which finishes first and recites their story without making mistakes wins.

relax	wash	kill	plan	visit
start	cry	hope	punish	smile
hike	dance	decide	pressure	stay
cycle	celebrate	enjoy	travel	stuff
view	watch	pray	climb	refuse
call	invite	promise	camp	stop
help	show	attend	laugh	experience

PRONUNCIATION ACTIVITY 8

Work with a partner. Adventurous Alexa and Shy Sandra are classmates. Tell what each of them did last year. Make as many sentences as you can by choosing from the lists below and by adding your own ideas.

Actions		Time Expressions	
stay home	talk to herself	most weekends	daily
hike with friends	learn to ski	almost every weekend	usually
talk to new people	travel to new cities	every day	seldom

Actions		Time Expressions	
plan to go out every day	date new people	as often as possible	occasionally
listen to music by herself	call up classmates	during the winter	almost never
watch videos alone in her apartment	like to have fun	in the evenings	whenever she could
walk in the park	try to meet new people	once in a while	frequently
clean the apartment	visit friends	always	often
taste new foods			

COMMUNICATING IN THE REAL WORLD

Use your English to talk to people outside your classroom. On your own or with a partner, talk to five people outside your class. Make up your own questions based on the topics in this chapter or ask the questions below and record the information.

Make a short report to the class about what you learned.

Here is one way to introduce your assignment.

> Could I ask you some questions? I am doing an assignment for my English class.

1. Compare this city now to what it was like 10 years ago.
2. How did the city change? What was the reason for that?
3. Do you like to travel? Why or why not? How many cities and countries have you visited?
4. What places would you like to visit?
5. Why is travel so popular these days?
6. What's your favourite way to travel?

SELF-EVALUATION

Think about your work in this chapter. For each row in the chart sections **Grammar and Language Functions**, **Learning Strategies**, and **Pronunciation**, give yourself a score based on the rating scale below and write a comment in the Notes section.

Show the chart to your teacher. Talk about what you need to do to make your English better.

Rating Scale

1	2	3	4	5

Needs improvement. ←——————————————→ *Great!*

	Score	Notes
Grammar and Language Functions		
narrating, talking about past events using the past tense and past progressive tense		
encouraging conversation		
describing past habits with *used to* and *would*		
giving explanations by stating reasons or stating results		
discussing similarities and differences using comparative and superlative forms		
paraphrasing		
Pronunciation		
correctly pronouncing the past tense endings of regular verbs		
Learning Strategies		
Speaking		
using signals such as *then*, *after that*, and *finally* to make it easier for the listener to understand when events happened		
controlling my nervousness and my emotions		
not being afraid to ask for help from others when I have problems expressing my ideas		
using synonyms or paraphrasing when I don't know or can't think of a word		

Listening		
listening for signals (*first*, *then*, *after that*) which tell the order in which things happened		
listening for numbers and signal words like *second* or *third* to help me understand details		

Vocabulary and Language Chunks

Look at this list of new vocabulary and language chunks you learned in this chapter. Give yourself a score based on the rating scale and write a comment.

to have no doubt	never a better time	to grow up
to go sightseeing	tourist attraction	to leave all that behind
to take home memories	to be home to	natural world
to go dancing	to take photographs	to fight for the underdog
to take a cruise	to go swimming	to be appalled
well worth visiting	up to date	to die off
to get going	second spot	to get to know
to bring something alive	to change the image of	to get in the way of
to be determined	the powers that be	to get someone

	Score	Notes
understanding new vocabulary and language chunks		
using new words and phrases correctly		

Write eight sentences and use new vocabulary you learned in this chapter.

1. _____

2. _____

3. _____

4. _____

5. _____

6. _____

7. _____

8. _____

My plan for practising is _____

_____

_____

_____

CHAPTER 3

Expanding Networks

Friends, Families, and Relationships

Requesting

Responding to requests

Making requests using indirect questions/statements

Asking for and giving information about present actions that started in the past

Getting time to think

Expressing necessity in the present

Expressing necessity in the past

Asking for and giving instructions to describe a process

THINKING AND TALKING

Discuss the following questions with a group.

1. Do you think friendship is important? Why?
2. What is your definition of a friend?
3. Someone once said "You can't choose your family but you can choose your friends." Which are more important to you—friends or family? Why?

LISTENING 1: THE IMPORTANCE OF FRIENDSHIP—A LECTURE

Before You Listen

👥 Pre-listening Vocabulary

A. You will hear a lecture on the audio CD that includes the following vocabulary. Work with a partner or by yourself to write the correct word next to its definition in the chart below.

relationship	aggressive	resource	to imitate
peer	to influence	emotional	effect
social	to function	security	collaboration
cognitive	benefit	researcher	cooperative

Definitions	Vocabulary
1. a person who is the equal of another person in position or age	*peer*
2. result	
3. connection between people and their behaviour and feelings towards each other	
4. to copy, mimic, be like	
5. relating to society and people	
6. act of working together	
7. having to do with knowing or understanding	
8. able to work well with others	
9. advantage; something good	
10. a person who studies or investigates	
11. a source or supply of help	
12. likely to attack or to hurt	
13. to change or affect	
14. dealing with feelings or emotions	
15. to serve as	
16. safety; feeling of safety	

B. Choose the correct vocabulary from the list above to fill in the blanks in these sentences. Use each word only once. Not all the words are used in the sentences. Please make changes to verbs or nouns when necessary.

1. Children like to learn from others who are like them, from their _____ **peers** _____.

2. Parents and teachers _____ children but not as much as other children do.

3. Children who are _____ don't have as many friends as children who are friendly.

4. Childhood friends have an impact on children's learning or _____ development.

5. We learn _____ skills from our friends.

6. Friendships give us a feeling of _____.

7. Friendships provide us with _____ support and teach us to handle our feelings.

8. Children get many _____ from friendship.

9. _____ learning occurs when we learn to solve problems together.

10. Our _____ or how we get along with other people help us to stay healthy and happy.

11. We all try to be like or _____ our friends sometimes.

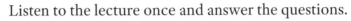

Pre-listening Activity

Work with a partner. You are going to hear how friendships affect children and adults. What do you think the speaker will say? Make three predictions.

1. _____
2. _____
3. _____

Listening STRATEGY

Listen for the main ideas. Usually the main ideas or points are repeated and emphasized.

Listening for the Main Ideas

Track 30

Listen to the lecture once and answer the questions.

1. Why are children's relationships important?
2. What does the speaker say about children's friendships, in general?
3. Were any of your predictions correct?

Listening Comprehension

Track 31

A. Listen to the lecture again. As you listen, number the sentences in the order in which the lecturer mentions them.

_____ First of all, friendships serve as emotional resources, both for having fun and for dealing with stress.

_____ Secondly, let's look at friends as cognitive resources. Children teach one another in many situations and are usually very good and effective in this activity.

_____ As emotional resources, friendships give children security.

__1__ The basics of friendship—close relationships and common interests—are first understood by children in early childhood.

_____ Indeed, childhood friendships teach us how to handle all our future relationships.

_____ Thirdly, let's turn to friends and social skills. A lot of evidence shows that both cooperation and conflict occur more in friendships than in other situations.

Track 32

B. Listen to the lecture again. Write *T* if the statement is true or *F* if it is false.

a. Children's school marks and classroom behaviour are the best predictors of how well they will do in their lives. _____

b. Close relationships and common interests are the basics of friendships. _____

c. Friendships give children a feeling of emotional security. _____

d. Friendships can help children and teenagers deal with stress. _____

e. Children don't learn very much from each other. _____

f. Peer modelling refers to children learning by working on tasks together. _____

g. Children only learn from each other by imitating each other. _____

h. Friendships help children develop social skills. _____

i. Children fight more often with their friends than with non-friends. _____

j. Friends are better teachers than non-friends. _____

k. Childhood friendships can't teach children about their future relationships. _____

l. Children who have friends are more skillful at getting along with other people. _____

Personalizing

Work in a group of four. Read the following quotation by Helen Keller. She was deaf and mute, and overcame her disability to become a famous teacher of the deaf.

> My friends have made the story of my life. In a thousand ways they have turned my limitations into beautiful privileges, and enabled me to walk serene and happy. . . .
>
> —Helen Keller

1. What do you think Helen Keller means by this?
2. Do you agree with her feelings about friendship? Please explain.
3. Discuss what you have learned from your friends.

VOCABULARY AND LANGUAGE CHUNKS

Write the number of each expression next to its meaning. After checking your answers, choose six expressions and write your own sentences.

Expressions

1. to have friends
2. to get along with
3. to have an influence on
4. to have fun
5. to care about each other
6. to solve problems
7. to deal with stress

Meanings

_____ to have the same interests
_____ to be like the others in the group
_____ to resolve differences
_____ to use as much time as necessary
_____ to enjoy oneself
_____ to feel affection and concern for each other
_____ to eliminate difficulties

8. to take time   _____ to handle or manage emotional or physical pressure

9. to work out differences   _____ to have an effect on

10. to fit in with the group   _____ to like and work well with

11. to share interests   __1__ to have relationships with people who like you

SPEAKING 1

Communication Focus 1: Requesting

English speakers make requests in three main ways:

1. Commands or imperatives: These can sound rude or angry depending on the tone of voice. Using *please* helps to soften the request.
   Examples:

   > **Close the door.**
   >
   > **Please close the door.**

2. Requests using modals (*could/would/can/will*): *Could/would* are considered more polite than *can/will*. There are two types of requests using modals.

   a. Direct requests:

   > **Can you spell your name, please?**
   >
   > **Could/Would you lend me your notes?**
   >
   > **Could you do me a favour? Would you change seats with me?**

   b. Indirect questions:

   > **I was wondering if you could lend me your notes?**

   If people think the request is a lot to ask, they will use a longer, indirect request.
   Examples:

   > **Would it be possible for me to borrow your car tomorrow afternoon?**
   >
   > **Could you possibly pick up the newspaper when you are at the store? I need it for my next class and I don't have time to get it myself.**
   >
   > **(The speaker thinks this a lot to ask and gives an explanation to soften the request.)**

3. Hints: There are no stated requests in hints. People understand from the context what the request is.
   Examples:

   > **It's very hot in here! (This could be a request to open the window.)**
   >
   > **Is that the doorbell? (This could be a request to answer the door.)**
   >
   > **Are there any cookies left? (This could be a request for a cookie.)**

SPEAKING ACTIVITY 1

Work with a partner. Make three requests to your teacher about three topics of your choice. Use the different kinds of requests. An example is given.

| Topic | Type of Request | | |
	Imperative	Direct Request	Hint
homework	Please don't give us a lot of homework today.	Could you please not give us a lot of homework today?	It's Anna's birthday today and we are all going to have a surprise party for her after school. We won't have time to do any homework.
1.			
2.			
3.			

Communication Focus 2: Responding to Requests

Some ways to respond to requests are listed below.

Positive	Negative
No problem.	Sorry, I can't . . .
Sure.	No, sorry.
Okay.	I don't think so.
	Maybe another time.
	It's not a good idea because . . .
Of course.*	I'm afraid not.*
Certainly.*	I'd rather not.*
I'd be glad to.*	I'm afraid that's impossible.*
With pleasure.*	

*These are more formal.

Grammar Note: Modals *can, will, could, would*

The modals *can, will, could,* and *would* are followed by the base form of the verb. However, *would you mind* requires the *-ing* ending (gerund) form of the verb because *mind* is a verb that requires a gerund.

SPEAKING ACTIVITY 2

Work in a group of three. In the following list, the requests and responses are mixed up. Identify all of the requests and write them in the chart. Then write the matching responses for each request. Put a plus sign (+) next to those expressions that you think are more formal and a minus sign (–) next to the ones you think are informal.

Excuse me, would you happen to have change for a twenty?	Could you run that by me again? What did you ask?
Could you tell me what that is?	Sure, no problem.
Speaking.	I asked what day it was.
Could I speak to Natalie?	I'm sorry, but I don't have one.
Would you mind my taking this seat?	I said the test's tomorrow.
Go ahead. I won't be using it for a while.	I'd be glad to. What do you want me to do?
Not at all. Please sit down.	Got change for a five?
Nope, sorry.	It's a stapler.
Could you do me a favour?	May I borrow your eraser?
Certainly. Will two tens do?	Can I give you a shout tomorrow?
I'm sorry, I didn't catch that. What did you say?	Could you possibly let me use your cellphone? I have an important call to make.

Requests	Responses
Excuse me, would you happen to have change for a twenty? +	Certainly, will two tens do? –

👥 SPEAKING ACTIVITY 3

Work with a partner. Make a list of five requests you could make to a friend and five requests you could make to an acquaintance. Choose the appropriate forms. Then practise requesting and responding. Do you notice any differences between requests in North America and requests in your country?

Requests to a close friend

1. _____
2. _____
3. _____
4. _____
5. _____

Requests to an acquaintance

1. _____
2. _____
3. _____
4. _____
5. _____

Communication Focus 3: Making Requests Using Indirect Questions/Statements

We use indirect questions when we want to be more polite or more formal.

Structures/Expressions	Examples
Do you know . . .	Do you know how many Facebook friends you have?
Can you tell me . . .	Can you tell me what friendship means to you?
Could you tell me . . .	Could you tell me how many Canadian friends you have?
I'd like to know . . .	I'd like to know if you are on Facebook.
Would you mind telling me . . .	Would you mind telling me what your email address is?

Grammar Note: Indirect Questions

We can use direct and indirect questions when making requests for information.

Direct questions use interrogative structures and word order.

Indirect questions/statements do not use interrogative structures and word order.

Indirect questions/statements are introduced by a phrase such as: *Could you tell me, please tell me,* and *I'd like to know . . . .*

Direct Questions	Indirect Questions
What kind of movies do you like?	I'd like to know what kind of movies you like.
When did you come to this school?	Would you mind telling me when you came to this school?
Where does he live?	I don't know where he lives.

Indirect statements beginning with *I don't know* are very common in conversation.

Examples:

> I don't know what you're talking about.
>
> I don't know why we're having problems.
>
> I don't know where he lives.

SPEAKING ACTIVITY 4

Work with a partner. Use indirect questions/statements to find out the answers to the following questions.

Example:

> **What is the name of your best friend?**
>
> **Question: Could you tell me what the name of your best friend is?**

1. Where does your friend live?

    Question:

    Answer:

2. What does he/she do for a living?

    Question:

    Answer:

3. What is he/she like?

    Question:

    Answer:

4. Where and when did you meet?

    Question:

    Answer:

5. What things do you like to do together?

    Question:

    Answer:

Speaking STRATEGY

When the listener doesn't understand or is having trouble following you, giving an example can make the meaning clearer.

SPEAKING ACTIVITY 5

Work with a partner. The following is a list of some of the qualities of a friend. Talk about friendship with your partner and decide together what you think are the five most important qualities in a best friend. Report your decisions to the class and give explanations.

outgoing	a good listener	romantic	secretive
friendly	interesting	good-looking	energetic
easy-going	kind	serious	independent
intelligent	trustworthy	optimistic	confident
funny	happy	enthusiastic	adventurous
loyal	stubborn	strong	

 SPEAKING ACTIVITY 6

Keep a record of the requests you make in the next week. Record three requests you make in the following locations. Bring your log to school and compare it with your partner's.

Location	Who did you make the request to?	What actual words did you use?	What was the response to your request?	Was your request successful? Why?
A store or business				
At school				
In your neighbourhood				

 SPEAKING ACTIVITY 7

Work with a partner. The following dialogues are not in order. First match the questions to the responses and then organize them so that they make up logical request dialogues. After that, practise saying the dialogues.

Speaking STRATEGY

If we think the request we are making is a lot of trouble to the listener, then we generally use longer, more complex requests, and often give an explanation.

1. James: Could you tell me how much the ticket is?

   James: Could you please tell me where Track 3 is?

   James: Could you please tell me how to get to Burlington.

   James: Would you happen to know when the next train is?

   James: Two tickets please. Would you have change for a fifty?

   Ticket agent: Certainly. Walk through the underpass and then you will see the sign for Track 3.

   Ticket agent: It's $5.00 for adults.

   Ticket agent: Sure, no problem.

   Ticket agent: You need to buy a ticket and take the train on Track 3.

   Ticket agent: The next one leaves at 4 o'clock.

2. Joe: What is it?

Felipa: I don't have any plans after school and I would be happy to give you a hand. There's just one thing.

Joe: Not at all. Of course I'll drive you home.

Felipa: If I stay after school, I'll miss my ride. Would you mind giving me a drive home after we finish working?

Joe: Hi, Felipa, how's it going?

Felipa: That's great. See you in the library after class.

Joe: Felipa, I was wondering if you are free after school and if you could help me with my presentation. Your English is so much better than mine.

Felipa: Just great. No complaints.

Communication Focus 4: Asking for and Giving Information about Present Actions That Started in the Past

We use the present perfect continuous (progressive) tense to describe actions that started in the past and are still true at the moment of speaking.

We use the present perfect continuous (progressive) tense to talk about how long an action has been going on.

Examples:

Samantha moved to Florida in 2014. She still lives in Florida.

Samantha <u>has been living</u> in Florida <u>since</u> 2014.

Erica started driving to work in 2014. She still drives to work.

Erica <u>has been driving</u> to work <u>since</u> 2014.

The Kims started speaking English when they moved to Toronto many years ago. They still speak English.

The Kims <u>have been speaking</u> English <u>for</u> many years. or

The Kims <u>have been speaking</u> English <u>since</u> they moved to Toronto.

Grammar Note: *for* or *since* with the Present Perfect Continuous (Progressive) Tense

We use *for* or *since* when talking about how long an action has been continuing. *For* tells the listener how long the action has continued: *for ten years, for three weeks, for a month.*

Since tells the listener when the action began: *since 2010, since last month, since Monday.*

We form the present perfect continuous (progressive) by using *have been* or *has been* + verb + *ing*.

Examples:

I *have been studying* English for a long time.

My friend Pierre *has been living* in Ottawa since September.

SPEAKING ACTIVITY 8

Work in a group of three. Make questions and find out how long each of you has been doing the following actions.

Actions	Me	Partner 1	Partner 2
Living in this city			
Studying at this school			
Speaking English			
Using social media			
Playing (any) sports or game			
Doing any other activity (for example: doing yoga, gardening, smoking, chewing your nails, driving to school, etc.)			

SPEAKING ACTIVITY 9

Make a quick chart with the headings shown below. Walk around the room and talk to at least eight classmates. Find out and record the following information. Report what you have discovered to the class.

Name	What's your favourite pastime?	How long have you been doing it?

Communication Focus 5: Getting Time to Think

Often we need time to think about the answers before we can answer a question. It's important to let the other person know that you plan to answer, but that you need some time to think. You can use some of these expressions—separately or together—to pause and organize your thoughts.

Hmm . . .	Let's see . . .	Okay.
Ahh . . .	Let me think . . .	Okay, well, let's see . . .
Well . . .	That's a good question.	

SPEAKING ACTIVITY 10

Work with a partner. Interview your partner about his or her ideas on friendship and people. Use the expressions above to give yourself time to think before you answer.

1. Is it easy for you to make friends? Why or why not?
2. Do your friends have any characteristics in common?
3. Do you have any childhood friendships that are still strong? How long have you been friends? Why has your friendship continued?
4. What new friends have you made in this city? Where and how did you meet them?
5. In what ways do your friends influence you? Who has influenced you the most in your life?
6. Can you forgive and forget if someone hurts you? What would make you stop being friends with someone?
7. Why do you think some people enjoy having friends and being with people while others prefer being alone? Which group do you belong to?
8. Do you have any heroes or heroines, people that you admire and look up to? Why do you admire them?
9. What do you expect from your friends?
10. What is the most important thing in friendship?
11. Who do you prefer to spend time with—your friends or your family?
12. How many Facebook friends do you have? Compare them to your other friends.

SPEAKING ACTIVITY 11

Working in a group of three, practise changing the direct questions below into indirect questions/statements. Use some of the following:

I'd like to know . . . ,

Please tell me . . .

Could you tell me . . . ,

Would you mind telling me . . .

Then interview each other using the indirect questions. Report three differences between you and your partners to the class.

Questions	Partner 1	Partner 2
What is your full name?	I'd like to know what your full name is.	
How many people were there in your family when you were growing up? What are the differences between families here and in your country?		
What kinds of things did your family like to do together?		
What is your happiest childhood memory?		
What chores or special jobs did you have when you were a child?		
What was your family life like when you were a teenager? What did you disagree with your parents about?		
How often and on what occasions does your family get together?		
What is the ideal family?		
Is family as important today as it used to be?		

LISTENING 2: CANADIAN FAMILIES— A NEWS REPORT

Before You Listen

👥 Pre-listening Vocabulary

A. You will hear a news report on the audio CD that includes the following vocabulary. Work with a partner or by yourself to write the correct word next to its definition in the chart below.

typical	proportion	reality	to challenge
traditional	minority	census	data
trend	common-law	makeup	apparently
to mark	couple		

Definitions	Vocabulary
1. two people who are together in a relationship, usually a man and a woman	*couple*
2. a part, share, or number in relation to the whole thing	
3. the real or true situation that exists	
4. the way something is put together or constructed	
5. to represent; to indicate; to be	
6. normal, average, usual	
7. the smaller part; less than half of the whole	
8. regular, customary, habitual, according to tradition	
9. a direction, style, or way in which things are changing	
10. to raise questions about; to disagree with	
11. it seems; it appears; it looks like	
12. an official counting of a population	
13. a collection of numerical information	
14. living together without being married to each other	

B. Choose the correct vocabulary from the list above to fill in the blanks in these sentences. Use each word only once. Not all the words are used in the sentences. Please make changes to verbs or nouns when necessary.

1. Our neighbours are a _____*couple*_____ from China.
2. The government conducts a _____ every few years to get information about people.
3. The _____ that they collect tell the government what people are doing.
4. The _____ or composition of the Canadian family is changing.
5. Married couples with children are less than 50 percent of the population. They are in the _____.
6. The _____ definition of the family no longer applies to all families because families have been changing.
7. The _____ is different from what many people think or believe to be true.
8. This census _____ the first time same-sex couples were counted.
9. Some people don't get married but they live together in a _____ relationship.

👥 Pre-listening Activity

1. Work with a partner. List as many different kinds of families as you can.
2. What do you know about families in Canada?
3. What are some questions that you have about families in Canada?

Compare your list with others in the class.

Listening for the Main Ideas

Listen to the report once and answer the questions.

1. What is the main topic of this interview?
2. Why are the speakers discussing this information?
3. How many of your questions were answered?

Listening STRATEGY 🎧
When you examine what you already know about a topic, your background knowledge, you will find the listening easier to understand.

Listening Comprehension

A. Listen to the report as many times as necessary and fill in the missing numbers in the sentences.

1. Before this census the typical Canadian family consisted of _____ adults and _____ children.
2. The year of the census was _____.
3. When counting married people, the census looked at people aged _____ and over.
4. In Newfoundland and Labrador _____ percent of people were married.
5. In Quebec _____ percent of people were married.
6. _____ percent of children live with a single parent.
7. _____ percent of marriages end in divorce.
8. _____ Canadians live in common-law relationships.
9. _____ percent of children live with common-law parents.
10. _____ percent of same-sex couples are married.

 **Track 35**

Listening STRATEGY

Monitor your understanding. What parts of the listening did you have trouble with?

B. Listen again and write *T* if the statement is true or *F* if it is false.

1. A new study tells us that the typical Canadian family has stayed the same. _____

2. The study says there are more married people than unmarried people in Canada. _____

3. The highest percentage of married people was in Newfoundland and Labrador. _____

4. The percentage of married people in Quebec is higher than in Newfoundland and Labrador. _____

5. There were more couples without children than with children. _____

6. Married couples with children number more than 50 percent of the population in all provinces. _____

7. Almost 20 percent of children live in single-parent families. _____

8. The fastest-growing families are common-law families. _____

9. This census did not report on same-sex marriage. _____

Personalizing

1. What is your reaction to the information you heard?
2. What surprised you the most?
3. What do you think the families of the future will look like?

VOCABULARY AND LANGUAGE CHUNKS

Write the number of each expression next to its meaning. After checking your answers, choose six expressions and write your own sentences.

Expressions	Meanings
1. to say "I do"	__1__ to get married
2. coast to coast	_____ younger than
3. end in	_____ increase quickly

4. a rain cloud   _____   to give information about

5. to report on   _____   two men or two women who are together as a couple

6. white picket fence   _____   no longer true

7. that loving feeling   _____   from one end of the country to the other

8. no longer apply   _____   finish in

9. under the age of   _____   to fall in love, to be in love

10. same-sex couple   _____   traditional family home with a white wooden fence around it

11. as far as something goes   _____   someone who brings bad news

12. grow fast   _____   to the degree that something exists; regarding, about something

SPEAKING 2

Communication Focus 6: Expressing Necessity in the Present

Structures/Expressions	Examples
It's necessary to . . .*	It's necessary to pay tuition fees. (You have no choice. You must do it.)
I must . . .*	I must pay tuition fees.
I have to . . .**	I have to pay tuition fees.
I've got to (have got to)**	I have got to pay tuition fees.

*used mostly in written or formal English
**used very often in conversation

Lack of Necessity

It isn't necessary to . . .   It isn't necessary to bring a gift.

He doesn't have to . . .   He doesn't have to work on Friday.

We don't have to . . .   We don't have to pay rent.

Question Forms

Is it necessary to . . .   Is it necessary to pay for the card?

Does he have to . . .   Does he have to take medicine?

Do we have to . . .   Do we have to sign a contract?

SPEAKING ACTIVITY 12

Work with a partner. Discuss three things you have to do and three things you don't have to do when you live with your family. Then talk about things you have to do and things you don't have to do when you live in a house or in an apartment.

Living with Your Family	
Things You Have to Do	**Things You Don't Have to Do**

Living in a House or an Apartment	
Things You Have to Do	**Things You Don't Have to Do**

Communication Focus 7:
Expressing Necessity in the Past

Structures/Expressions	Examples
It was necessary to . . .	It was necessary to pay tuition fees. (You had no choice. You did it.)
I had to . . .	I had to pay tuition fees.
Lack of Necessity	
It wasn't necessary to . . .	It wasn't necessary to bring a gift.
He didn't have to . . .	He didn't have to bring a gift.
Question Forms	
Was it necessary to . . .	Was it necessary to take the medicine?
Did he/we have to . . .	Did he have to take the medicine?

SPEAKING ACTIVITY 13

Read the following blog entry about "the roommate from hell." Then list some advantages and disadvantages of living with a roommate. Use *have to* and *don't have to*. Compare your answers with a partner.

> My roommate from hell made potatoes every day for dinner. Oh, but *how* did she make them? She put potatoes and water in a pan, and put the burner on the highest setting. After the water boiled over, and coated the burner with a sticky, slimy mess, she used to turn it down and that mess hardened on the stove. Then she would take her meal into the living room and plunk herself in front of the TV and slurp loudly as she ate. After eating, she rinsed her dishes and the saucepan in cold water (no soap), and put them back in the cupboard. And that was the ONLY cleaning she ever did. She used to borrow my food, my clothes, and my beer, and I would never see these items again. And if I said anything, she would explode. She had a terrible temper. She used to call my friends awful names. Piles of clothing, books, and garbage used to litter the apartment we shared. I finally couldn't take any more and moved out!

SPEAKING ACTIVITY 14

Work with a partner. Make up a list of things you had to do when you were in high school and things you didn't have to do. Then think about the lives of your great-grandparents 100 years ago. Make a list of things they had to do and things they didn't have to do.

When You Were a High School Student	
Things You Had to Do	**Things You Didn't Have to Do**

Your Great-Grandparents	
Things They Had to Do	**Things They Didn't Have to Do**

SPEAKING ACTIVITY 15

Work with a partner. Tell your partner about four things you had to do before you came to this country. Try to use *first, next, then,* and *finally* in your answers.

Communication Focus 8: Asking for and Giving Instructions to Describe a Process

Asking for Information

Structures/Expressions	Examples
Can/could you explain . . .	Could you explain how to fill in the form?
Do you know how to . . .	Do you know how to set the burglar alarm?
Please show me how to . . .	Please show me how to program the thermostat.
How does . . . work?	How does this appliance work?

Describing a Process

When we describe a process we often use sequence markers to clearly outline the steps and the order in which they occur.

Sequence Markers	Example: Making a Snowman
First	First, you have to pack snow into a snowball. Make the ball bigger by rolling it in the snow on the ground over and over until the ball is big enough to be the base for your snowman. Put the base on the spot where you want the snowman to stand.
Then	Then, make the middle section by repeating the first step, but the ball should be slightly smaller. Place the middle ball on top of the first ball or base.
Next	Next, repeat step one to make the snowman's head. This ball has to be smaller than the other two. Place the third ball on top of the middle ball.
After that	After that, make the snowman's eyes by putting two pieces of charcoal on the head. Use a carrot for his nose. Cut small dots out of fabric and use this to form a mouth. Put a scarf or tie around the snowman's neck. Put sticks into the middle section for arms and put mittens on the ends of the sticks. Finish the snowman by adding a hat.

| Finally, at the end | Finally, make your snowman special. Put some interesting clothes on your snowman or add some props, like skis, a broom or shovel, or some stuffed animals. Give your snowman personality. |

SPEAKING ACTIVITY 16

Work with a partner. Read the following instructions for removing ink from clothing. How many steps are there? What are they? What are the sequence markers?

How to Remove Black Ink from a Garment

First, spray the stain with hairspray. Let it sit for a while and then try to sponge the ink out. If that does not work, try rubbing alcohol next. Put alcohol on the stain and sponge it off. As a last resort, try milk. After that, wash according to instructions. The stain should go away.

Choose three of the following topics and describe the steps necessary to complete the task.

1. How to address an envelope
2. How to fill a bicycle tire with air
3. How to make an omelette or other dish
4. How to make friends
5. How to improve your English

SPEAKING ACTIVITY 17

Think about a process you know how to do very well. Write out the steps. Then get together with another two students and teach each other your processes.

PRONUNCIATION

Pronunciation Focus:
Intonation Patterns for Questions and Statements

Intonation is the rising and falling of the pitch of the voice when we are speaking. Intonation patterns are important in English because they carry meaning. Intonation patterns tell the listener if the speaker has finished speaking or if the speaker is waiting for an answer. Intonation carries almost as much meaning as vocabulary or grammar.

Common Intonation Patterns

1. *Yes/No* **Questions: Rising** intonation is used when people are uncertain, or when they are asking questions. *Yes/No* questions have rising intonation. The pitch of the voice rises on the last stressed syllable of the sentence.

    > Were they happy?

    > Could I borrow your dictionary?

2. **Statements and Commands:** Statements have a **rising–falling** intonation. Rising–falling intonation tells the listener that the speaker has finished speaking. In rising–falling intonation, the voice rises on the last stressed syllable of the sentence and then falls to its lowest pitch level.

    > They conducted a survey.

    > The children went to the movie.

    > Please leave the room.

3. *Wh-* **Questions:** We use **rising–falling** intonation with *wh-* questions which begin with question words such as *what, where, when, why,* and *how*. Indirect questions also take rising–falling intonation

    > Where are you going?

    > When will you be finished?

    > Please tell me where you live.

    > Could you tell me where John is.

4. When we use *wh-* questions to ask someone to repeat, to ask for clarification, or to express surprise, we can also use rising intonation. The intonation starts to go up on the question word and rises at the end of the question.

    > I'm looking for a new roommate.

    > What did you say?

    > I need a new roommate. Georgette moved out.

5. We can use rising intonation to ask for confirmation

    > First, I turn off the alarm, and then I unlock the door. Right?

 PRONUNCIATION ACTIVITY 1

Track 36

A. Listen to this conversation. Decide if the intonation pattern for each of the phrases is rising or falling. Put a check mark in the correct column.

	Phrases	Rising →	Falling →
Person A:	Front desk?		
Person B:	Wake up call, please.		
Person A:	What time?		
Person B:	Quarter past six.		
Person A:	Six?		
Person B:	Quarter past six.		
Person A:	Okay.		

B. Now listen again and check your answers.

C. Check your answers with a partner and the teacher.

PRONUNCIATION ACTIVITY 2

A. Listen to the sentences and mark the intonation pattern on each one. Use rising arrows ⤻ for *Yes/No* questions and rising–falling arrows ⌒⤻ for final rising–falling intonation.

 Track 37

I'm still hungry.	In the fridge.
What do you feel like?	I'm starving!
Take as many as you want.	How many can I have?
You're welcome.	Tons!
Where are they?	What?
Are there any cupcakes left?	Thanks.

B. Check your answers with a partner. Then arrange the sentences into a conversation and practise saying it with your partner.

PRONUNCIATION ACTIVITY 3

A. Listen to each sentence, and then repeat it.

 Track 38

1. What are the benefits of friendships?
2. What do we get from them?
3. I was wondering if I could borrow your notes?
4. What time is it?
5. Could you tell me how much the ticket costs?
6. Friendships provide children with ways of developing basic social skills.
7. Can I renew these books?

8. Did you learn a lot about relationships?
9. Could I talk to you for a moment?
10. Is anything wrong?
11. Do you have change for a twenty?
12. What did you say?

B. Practise saying the sentences with a partner.

PRONUNCIATION ACTIVITY 4

Track 39

A. Mark the intonation patterns on these sentences.

1. **Can I borrow your books?**

2. **Where are they?**

3. Excuse me, would you happen to have change for a twenty?

4. Could you tell me what that is?

5. You're welcome.

6. Could I speak to Natalie?

7. Would you mind my taking this seat?

8. Can I give you a shout tomorrow?

9. Please tell me what your name is.

10. Could you run that by me again?

11. I'm sorry, I didn't catch that.

12. What did you say?

13. Could you do me a favour?

14. Could I possibly use your cellphone?

15. Got change for a five?

16. May I borrow your eraser?

B. Now listen to the sentences to check your answers.

C. Practise saying the sentences with your partner.

PRONUNCIATION ACTIVITY 5

Work with a partner. Ask each other four *Yes/No* questions and four *wh-* questions. Listen to make sure your partner is using the right intonation.

PRONUNCIATION ACTIVITY 6

Work in a group of four. Brainstorm a list of questions about friends, family, or housing that you could ask the other people in your class. When you have a list, each person will choose three different questions. Write out your sentences and draw intonation patterns, and practise asking your questions. Walk around the room and ask as many people as possible. Then get back together with another group and report what you found out.

PRONUNCIATION ACTIVITY 7

A. Listen to this recipe for a favourite snack—roasted almonds. Fill in the missing information.

Track 40

This is what you need:

_____ cups of almonds (or 1 pound or 500 grams)

_____ tablespoon (or _____) of olive oil

_____ teaspoons (or _____) of sea salt

_____ teaspoons of hot or mild paprika

This is what you do:

_____, _____ a baking sheet with foil or parchment.

_____, in a large _____, toss the almonds with salt, oil, and _____.

_____, _____ them evenly on a baking _____.

_____, roast the almonds in a _____ oven for about _____ minutes, until they are lightly toasted, and then cool and _____.

B. Check your answers with a partner. Use expressions for checking confirmation such as *Right?* and *Okay?*.

C. Write out your own recipe for something good to eat and tell your partner the steps.

D. Read your partner's recipe to the class. After each pair has had a turn, the class will vote for the tastiest food.

COMMUNICATING IN THE REAL WORLD

Use your English to talk to people outside your classroom. On your own or with a partner, talk to five people outside your class. Make up your own questions based on the topics in this chapter or ask the questions below and record the information.

Make a short report to the class about what you learned.

Here is one way to introduce your assignment.

Could I ask you some questions? I am doing an assignment for my English class.

1. What is your definition of a friend?
2. Where does your best friend live?
3. What do you like doing with your best friend?
4. What's your favourite pastime? How long have you been doing it?
5. How long have you been living in this city?
6. Are you on Facebook? How many Facebook friends do you have?
7. What do you think families will look like in the future?

SELF-EVALUATION

Think about your work in this chapter. For each row in the chart sections **Grammar and Language Functions**, **Learning Strategies**, and **Pronunciation**, give yourself a score based on the rating scale below and write a comment in the Notes section.

Show the chart to your teacher. Talk about what you need to do to make your English better.

Rating Scale

1	2	3	4	5

Needs improvement. ←————————————————————→ *Great!*

	Score	Notes
Grammar and Language Functions		
making and responding to requests		
making requests using commands, modals, indirect questions, or hints		
using expressions to give myself time to think before answering		
asking for and giving information about present actions that started in the past		
using *since* and *for* with the present perfect continuous (progressive) tense		
expressing necessity and lack of necessity in the present		
expressing necessity and lack of necessity in the past		
asking for and giving instructions to describe a process		
Pronunciation		
using the correct intonation patterns with questions and statements		

Learning Strategies

Speaking

using longer, more complex requests, and giving an explanation if the request I am making is a lot of trouble to the listener		
giving an example to make my meaning clearer when the listener doesn't understand or is having trouble following me		

Listening

listening for the main ideas or points that are repeated and emphasized		
examining what I already know about a topic (my background knowledge), to help make the listening easier to understand		
monitoring my understanding and asking myself what parts of the listening I had trouble with		

Vocabulary and Language Chunks

Look at this list of new vocabulary and language chunks you learned in this chapter. Give yourself a score based on the rating scale and write a comment.

to have friends	to fit in with the group	end in
to get along with	to share interests	a rain cloud
to have an influence on	to solve problems	white picket fence
to spend time	to care about each other	that loving feeling
to have fun	to say "I do"	no longer apply
to deal with stress	coast to coast	under the age of
to take time	to work out differences	same-sex couple
as far as something goes	grow fast	

	Score	Notes
understanding new vocabulary and language chunks		
using new words and phrases correctly		

Write eight sentences and use new vocabulary you learned in this chapter.

1. _____
2. _____
3. _____
4. _____
5. _____
6. _____
7. _____
8. _____

My plan for practising is _____

_____

_____

_____

_____

CHAPTER 4

Living the Good Life

Food and Lifestyles

Talking about events in the indefinite past

Expressing likes and dislikes

Stating opinions; agreeing, disagreeing and supporting opinions

THINKING AND TALKING

Work with a partner to label the following statements about food as *true* or *false*. Discuss your answers with the class.

Statement	True	False
1. There is more sugar in lemons than in strawberries.		
2. The staple diet of more than 50 percent of the world's population is rice.		
3. People have found the remains of food take-out stores or fast-food shops in ancient Greek ruins.		
4. An average person eats about 35 tons of food during her or his lifetime.		
5. Ice cream originally comes from China. When Marco Polo returned to Italy from China in 1295, one of the things he brought back was a recipe for "ice milk," which later developed into ice cream.		
6. In France, people eat approximately 500 million snails every year.		
7. In the past, salt was very rare and extremely valuable. People were often paid their wages in salt. The word *salary* comes from *salt*.		
8. Frozen fruits and vegetables are sometimes more nutritious than fresh fruits and vegetables.		
9. If you are cold, you are more likely to feel hungry. Temperature affects our appetites.		
10. It takes about 3,500 calories to make a pound of fat.		
11. Peanuts are used in the making of dynamite.		
12. In the Middle Ages, people believed that the juice of a lemon could dissolve fish bones, and that is why fish is often served with a slice of lemon.		

Which of the above statements do you find the most surprising? Explain why.

SPEAKING 1

Communication Focus 1:
Talking about Events in the Indefinite Past

We often give information about events in the past with no specific
past time reference. We can use adverbs such as *ever, always, never,
occasionally, often, several times,* and *recently* to express this indefiniteness.
Examples:

Have you ever eaten snake?	No I haven't, but I've eaten frogs' legs.
Has she ever drunk champagne?	No she hasn't, but she's drunk beer.

I have never had Indonesian food.

We have always had cereal for breakfast.

I have lost 20 lbs (9 kilos) recently!

Grammar Note: Present Perfect Tense for Actions in the Indefinite Past

We use the present perfect tense to talk about an action in the past when
there is no specific past time reference. To form the present perfect tense,
use *have/has* + past participle.
Examples:

Have you had lunch yet?

Ellen has often eaten Chinese food.

My friends have never been to Italy.

SPEAKING ACTIVITY 1

Walk around the room and talk to as many students as necessary until
you find someone who has done the specific action in the table below.
Make questions using "Have you ever . . . ?" When you find someone who
fits the description in one of the boxes, write down his or her name. Then
ask the person when and where they did that action. You may write each
person's name only once.

Speaking STRATEGY

When you ask or answer
questions, try to use
complete sentences.
This will help you
develop fluency.

Find someone who . . .	Question	Name	Where/When
. . . has had Italian food.	Have you ever had Italian food?	Tina	She had Italian food at a restaurant last week.
. . . has eaten snake.			
. . . has had rabbit.			
. . . has gone to a vegetarian restaurant.			
. . . has eaten Korean food.			
. . . has had ginseng tea.			
. . . has eaten snails.			
. . . has had food from an African country.			
. . . has tried chicken wings.			
. . . has bought food at a farmers' market.			
. . . has eaten any kind of insect.			
. . . has drunk espresso.			
. . . has tried sushi or sashimi.			
. . . has baked a birthday cake.			
. . . has gone to a potluck meal.			
. . . has roasted a turkey.			

SPEAKING ACTIVITY 2

What are the most unusual foods in the world? Work with a partner. The following list describes some unusual foods from different countries. Which of these foods have you tried? Choose the three foods that you think are the most unusual. Then choose the three foods that you would like to try and the three foods that you would never try. Compare your ideas to those of another pair of students.

Live octopus (South Korea)

The octopus is served alive and moving. People who like this dish recommend eating it quickly.

Grasshoppers (Uganda)

During the rainy season, you can buy grasshoppers at the local markets. They can be cooked or raw, and you can buy them with or without wings and legs.

Pigeon (France)

Pigeon is an expensive dish served in some of the best restaurants in France. It has a strong flavour and is popular in many parts of the world.

Durian (Malaysia)

This is a fruit with a very strong, stinky odour that some people have compared to the smell of rotting garbage. This spiky fruit may not be popular with foreigners but many Malaysians love it.

Grubs (Australia)

These white grubs are the larvae of moths and are very high in protein. They make a tasty snack. They were once an important food and a part of the diet of Aboriginal people living in the deserts of Australia.

Camel (Somalia, Saudi Arabia, and Egypt)

Camel can provide a large quantity of meat. The brisket, ribs, and loin are some of the better parts, but the hump is the best part. Camel meat tastes like beef.

Snake wine (Vietnam)

Some people say that snake wine has health benefits. It is an alcoholic drink made using snake blood, with a snake (or sometimes another creature such as a scorpion) inside the bottle. It is best to drink this strong cocktail quickly.

Donkey (Italy)

In Italy, donkey meat is eaten much like Italian ham. People can easily get this meat in bars.

Buffalo/Bison (North America)

Bison (sometimes called buffalo) meat is used in North America because it has only 10–12 percent fat. It is a source of protein, and many vitamins and minerals. People can use it in any recipe that calls for beef.

Ostrich (South Africa)

Ostrich is low in cholesterol and is considered healthier than other meats. It is popular all over the world. People eat everything from ostrich burgers to omelettes made from ostrich eggs.

Fried tarantulas (Cambodia)

These huge, deadly spiders are sold at roadside stands and then fried with garlic. The legs are crispy but the stomach and internal organs are very gooey.

The Three Most Unusual Foods	Three Foods We Would Like to Try	Three Foods We Will Never Try

Communication Focus 2: Expressing Likes and Dislikes

Expressing Likes

Verbs	Examples
to like	John likes having seafood for dinner.
to love	His friends love to eat sushi.
to enjoy	Melissa really enjoys having lobster.
to feel like	Terry feels like going out to eat tonight.

Structures/Expressions	Examples
to be fond of . . .	I am really fond of eating Chinese food. We are fond of diet drinks.
to be crazy about . . .	Sherry is crazy about chocolate. She wants to have it all the time.
. . . is my favourite	Yogurt is my favourite snack.

Expressing Dislikes

Verbs	Examples
(not) to care for	Joanna doesn't care for asparagus.
(not) to like	Abbas doesn't like turnips.
can't stand	Mary Ann can't stand eating raw fish.
to hate	My friend hates to eat leftovers.
to detest	Andrea detests spicy food.
to avoid	Mike avoids eating fried food.

Structures/Expressions	Examples
. . . to turn off	The smell of fish turns him off.
. . . to be put off by	Janet is put off by smelly cheeses.

Grammar Note: Verbs Taking Both Gerunds and Infinitives

The verbs *like*, *love*, *hate*, and *can't stand* can be followed by a gerund (base form of the verb + *-ing*) or by an infinitive (*to* + base form of the verb).
Examples:

I love eating out.

I love to eat out.

Her roommate hates doing the dishes.

Her roommate hates to do the dishes.

Other verbs such as *enjoy* and *avoid* can only be followed by a gerund or a noun. Expressions such as *to be fond of . . .*, *to be crazy about . . .*, and *to care for . . .* end in prepositions, and these can only be followed by a noun or a gerund.
Examples:

Thelma enjoys having dessert. Her sister Anita doesn't care for sweets, so she usually avoids eating dessert.

Martin is fond of eating sushi.

Jennifer is allergic to peanuts. She avoids eating foods with peanuts in them.

👥 SPEAKING ACTIVITY 3

Work with a partner. Interview your partner using the questions below. Report the most interesting information to the class.

1. Do you live to eat or do you eat to live?
2. What is your favourite junk food? How often do you eat it?
3. What food or drink are you crazy about?
4. What food or drink do you avoid having? Explain.
5. What foods are you fond of? Please explain why.
6. What are some foods you don't care for?
7. What foods from your country do you miss having here?
8. What was your favourite food and drink when you were a child?
9. How does the food in your country compare to the food here? Which do you prefer to eat?
10. Do you like to try unusual foods or drinks? Why?
11. What fruits do you love eating?
12. What snacks do you enjoy having?
13. Is there anything you feel like having now?

Speaking STRATEGY 💬

When you are answering questions, check to see if the listener understands by asking questions such as "Are you following me?", "Do you know what I mean?", and "Do you understand?".

LISTENING 1: LIKES AND DISLIKES IN FOOD—A DISCUSSION

Before You Listen

👥 Pre-listening Vocabulary

A. You will hear a discussion on the audio CD that includes the following vocabulary. Work with a partner or by yourself to write the correct word next to its definition in the chart below.

peculiar	irrational	texture	craving
compound	behaviour	biological	toxins
slimy	preference	to interfere	to override
nutrition	idiosyncrasy	nutrient	
heartburn	finicky	avoidance	

Definitions	Vocabulary
1. the taking in of food and drink which is used for energy, growth, and repair	nutrition
2. unusual, strange	
3. fussy, not easily pleased	
4. the way a person acts and behaves	
5. act of staying away from, avoiding	
6. how the surface of something looks or feels	
7. a mixture	
8. something that nourishes	
9. to get in the way of	
10. poisons	
11. a favourite, a preferred thing	
12. to be more important than	
13. uncomfortable burning feeling in the lower part of the chest; indigestion	
14. a very strong desire	
15. slippery; wet and greasy	
16. unconventional, unusual behaviour	
17. relating to biology or living things; natural qualities present from birth	
18. not reasonable, not logical	

B. Choose the correct vocabulary from the list above to fill in the blanks in these sentences. Use each word only once. Not all the words are used in the sentences. Please make changes to verbs or nouns when necessary.

1. Proper _____nutrition_____ is very important for your health.

2. Many people have a _____ for sweet foods over salty foods.

3. There are not many _____ in sweets.

4. He doesn't eat everything. He's very _____.

5. People have different individual habits or _____ when it comes to eating or not eating certain foods.

6. Sometimes there is a _____ or health reason for liking or disliking certain foods.

7. People's reactions to foods can be very _____ or unreasonable.

8. She has an allergy to fish and that's the reason for her _____ of fish and fish products.

9. She eats chocolate all the time. She has a strong _____ for it.

10. Don't eat that dish. It has a _____ smell and taste.

🖎 Pre-listening Activity

A. Work with a partner. Talk about two foods you don't like to eat.

B. You are going to listen to a discussion on the audio CD about why people have certain likes and dislikes in food. Write down two questions you have about this topic. Discuss your questions with a partner.

1. _____

2. _____

Listening for the Main Ideas

Listen to the discussion once, and then answer the questions.

 Track 41

1. What kind of show is this and why are the guests there?

2. What are some strange food behaviours that they discuss?

3. According to the discussion, why do people have likes and dislikes in food?

4. Did you find answers to your two questions above? What did you learn?

> **Listening STRATEGY** 🕮
>
> Listen for definitions or explanations to help you understand new or difficult words. Often a definition follows an unusual or difficult word, to explain or clarify meaning. For example, in the phrase "your preferences, your likes and dislikes . . .," the word *preferences* is explained by what follows.

Listening for Comprehension

 **Track 42**

A. Listen to the discussion again. As you listen, write out the definitions/explanations/examples that the speakers give for the listed words and phrases.

crazy about cucumbers	_loves to eat them_
a food aversion	_____
finicky or picky eaters	_____
idiosyncratic food behaviours	_____
nutrients	_____
supertasters	_____
originate	_____
the toddler years	_____
phobias	_____

 **Track 43**

B. Now, listen to the discussion again and answer the questions.

1. What foods does Dr. Wu dislike?
2. What is one reason people don't eat red meat or other high-protein foods?
3. Why do some people dislike green foods?
4. Why do we prefer to eat certain foods?
5. What are supertasters?
6. How do parents pass on their food likes and dislikes to their children?

Personalizing

With a partner, discuss some idiosyncratic food behaviours you each have and try to find an explanation for them.

VOCABULARY AND LANGUAGE CHUNKS

Write the number of each expression next to its meaning. After checking your answers, choose six expressions and write your own sentences.

Expressions	**Meanings**
1. the sight of	_____ no problem
2. to break up with	_____ to keep away from; to avoid something you dislike or fear
3. to shy away from	_____ to let something go by; not to take
4. high up on the list	_____ probably will

5. to warn about _____ close to the top of the list in importance

6. likely to _____ to give to somebody

7. to pass on to someone _____ to choose

8. to pick out _____ to be ready to accept new things; to be open

9. to pass up _____ to give a warning or to caution about

10. to open up to _____ from another point of view

11. no worries _____ to take actions to fix or to make better

12. to make up for _____ to end a romantic relationship with

13. to do something about _____ to compensate for

14. on the other hand __1__ the appearance of

SPEAKING 2

Communication Focus 3: Stating Opinions; agreeing, disagreeing and supporting opinions

Here are some phrases you can use to express your opinions and ideas:

Structures/Expressions	Examples
(Personally) I feel/believe/think*	I personally feel that yoga is good for you.
In my opinion/view . . .	In my opinion, traditional Chinese medicine can make you feel better.
As far as I'm concerned . . .	As far as I'm concerned, a positive attitude improves your health.
I am certain/sure/positive that . . .	I am positive that cooking destroys some of the nutrients in food.
If you ask me, . . .	If you ask me, fast food is responsible for many illnesses.
Here's my two cents' worth.	Here's my two cents' worth. Exercising is the most important thing you can do for your health.

*Using *I think* to express an opinion is very common in conversations in North America.

You can use these structures/expressions to ask for opinions:

What's your idea?   How do you feel?

What do you think/believe?   What's your opinion?

Agreeing with Opinions

Diplomatic/Tactful/ Less Certain	Neutral	Very Certain/Positive
That's true.	I believe you are right.	Exactly! Of course!
You have a point.	I agree.	Absolutely!
Okay.	That's how I feel, too.	That's right!/right on!
All right.	I think so, too.	That goes without saying!

Disagreeing with Opinions

Diplomatic/Tactful/ Less Certain	Neutral	Very Certain/Positive
I'm not sure I agree.	I don't agree.	Absolutely not!
I'm afraid I don't agree.	I don't think that's right.	I totally disagree. No way!

Supporting Opinions

Speaking STRATEGY

Encourage yourself. You can be just as good as others at getting your message across.

There are a number of ways that you can support your opinions.

1. You can strengthen or support your opinion by giving reasons.
2. You can support your opinion by stating facts and experiences.
3. You can support your opinions by stating what experts or authorities say.

SPEAKING ACTIVITY 4

Work with a partner. Read these questions and express your opinions. Try to find support for your opinions. Then get together with another pair of students and talk about your agreements and disagreements.

1. Do you believe that there is a direct connection between the food we eat and the diseases we get? Please explain.
2. Why are there so many more obese people in North America than in other countries?
3. Do you think that people who take risks with their health (e.g., smokers, alcoholics, extreme sports enthusiasts, the obese, etc.) should be asked to pay more for health care?
4. Do you think smoking should be illegal? Why or why not?
5. Do you think that a positive attitude has an effect on your health?
6. Researchers say that love and marriage help people live longer. Do you agree?
7. Do you think that laughter is "the best medicine"?

8. Do you believe that people have the right to choose to die?

9. Do you believe in mind over matter—that the mind has the power to cure illness?

10. Do you think that in the future people will live to be at least 150 years old?

11. What part of the world is the best to live in from a health point of view?

LISTENING 2: EXERCISE AND HEALTH— A CBC NEWS REPORT

Before You Listen

👥 Pre-listening Vocabulary

A. You will hear a news report on the audio CD that includes the following vocabulary. Work with a partner or by yourself to write the correct word next to its definition in the chart below.

evidence	heart disease	detectable	to investigate
clinical	stroke	beneficial	to recommend
solid	diabetes	breakdown	to advocate
findings	to analyze	patient	to incorporate
particularly	trials	effective	to accumulate
moderate	vigorous	to reduce	treatment
medication			

Definitions	Vocabulary
1. firm, hard; strong	solid
2. to make less	
3. can be seen or noticed; noticeable	
4. good; of benefit; useful	
5. related to work with patients; in a clinic	
6. medical care given to a patient	
7. to say something is suitable or desirable for a certain purpose or use	
8. to speak or write in favour of; to support something	
9. facts or information which prove something	
10. something a doctor prescribes to treat an illness; medicine	
11. results of research	
12. a person who gets medical treatment from a doctor	

continued on next page

Definitions	Vocabulary
13. especially	
14. average, reasonable; not too much or too little	
15. strong, energetic, forceful	
16. an illness; disease of the heart	
17. sudden death of brain cells when blood to that part of the brain is blocked	
18. a disease in which the body cannot control the sugar in the blood because it does not have enough insulin	
19. to study something, to learn about its parts	
20. medical studies to see how effective a treatment or a medicine is	
21. information separated into different groups	
22. to examine, study, or search	
23. to include as part of a whole	
24. to collect or gather together	
25. successful in producing a desired result	

B. Choose the correct vocabulary from the list above to fill in the blanks in these sentences. Use each word only once. Not all the words are used in the sentences. Please make changes to verbs or nouns when necessary.

1. There is _____ solid _____ evidence that says exercise can be as good as medicine for certain diseases.

2. The researchers did hundreds of _____ or studies to find out if medication was better than exercise.

3. The _____ from the studies shows that exercise can be better or more _____ than drugs.

4. The researchers say they need to do more _____ studies to be sure about these results.

5. A British doctor told _____ not to stop taking their _____.

6. These days doctors advise or _____ that heart patients exercise as well as take medications.

7. Doctors are not _____ that people throw away their medicines.

8. They are telling people _____ exercise into their daily routines.

9. Health Canada recommends that people build up or _____ 150 minutes of exercise per week.

10. Doctors want to _____ the benefits of exercise by doing more studies.

11. Working out hard or doing _____ exercise can be _____ for many different conditions.

🎧 Pre-listening Activity

Work in a small group. Brainstorm all the things that you believe are part of a healthy lifestyle. Choose someone to present your ideas to the class. Use opinion statements and support your opinions. The audience can use statements of agreement and disagreement.

Listening STRATEGY 👂
As you listen, formulate questions about points that are not clear to you. This will help make the meaning clear when you discuss these points later.

Listening for the Main Ideas

Listen to the news report once. Check off the main ideas you hear discussed.

 Track 44

1. Exercise can be as effective as drugs in treating some diseases. ☐
2. Patients' diets can affect their health. ☐
3. There are studies which compare exercise and drugs in treating certain illnesses. ☐
4. There are many different kinds of prescription drugs and medications. ☐
5. Doctors should prescribe physical activity. ☐
6. Health Canada recommends certain amounts of exercise for adults and children. ☐

Listening Comprehension

Listen to the news report again. Write *T* if the statement is true or *F* if it is false.

Track 45

1. Exercise can be just as effective as medicine for some diseases. _____T_____
2. The researchers studied people in Canada and the US. _____
3. The studies involved 314,000 people. _____
4. The studies showed no differences between exercise and drugs in reducing the risk of death in all illnesses. _____
5. For diabetes and for stroke and heart disease, exercise was better than medication alone. _____
6. Researchers say they need to do more studies about the effects of exercise. _____
7. The researchers say that doctors need to prescribe exercise for patients. _____
8. A British health expert says heart patients can stop taking medications completely. _____
9. Health Canada says adults should do two and a half hours of exercise every day. _____
10. The World Health Organization says that physical inactivity causes 32 million deaths a year. _____

Personalizing

A. Work with a partner. What are your opinions about the following? Do you agree with each other? Try to support your opinions.

Topic	My Opinion	My Partner's Opinion
The best kinds of physical activity		
Taking a lot of medications		
The best way to look after your health		
How to avoid getting sick		
The best way to handle stress		

B. With your partner make a mind map of a healthy lifestyle. Tell each other what you think are the three most important elements.

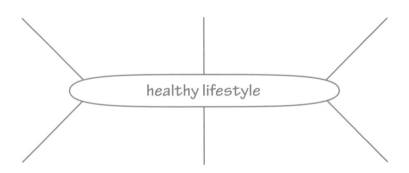

VOCABULARY AND LANGUAGE CHUNKS

Write the number of each expression next to its meaning. After checking your answers, choose six expressions and write your own sentences.

Expressions

1. prescription drugs
2. to throw away
3. to back up
4. physical activity

Meanings

__1__ medicine which you can only buy with a doctor's prescription

_____ said in a different way

_____ to keep well; to keep in good health

_____ in danger of

5. risk factor   _____ that will be enough

6. to start out   _____ to walk up the stairs

7. as simple as that   _____ to begin

8. to take the stairs   _____ energetic bodily movement

9. that'll do it   _____ as easy, as uncomplicated as that

10. at risk of   _____ anything that increases the possibility of illness or death

11. to stay healthy   _____ not to keep; to get rid of

12. in other words   _____ to give additional supporting facts

13. to look into   _____ to go for a walk

14. to take a walk   _____ to examine or study more

SPEAKING ACTIVITY 5

Work with a partner. Interview each other. Discuss these questions using opinion statements and report the two most interesting facts to the class.

1. Are you afraid of going to the doctor or the dentist? What is the reason for your fear?

2. Have you ever been in the hospital? How long did you stay? How did you feel about it?

3. What disease are you most afraid of?

4. Do you take garlic, ginseng, or other herbs or medicines to cure or prevent illness? Why or why not?

5. Why do you think women live longer than men?

6. Why do so many more people get cancer and Alzheimer's disease than ever before? What can be done to prevent this?

7. According to the World Health Organization, about 3,000 people commit suicide every day. Why are so many people committing suicide?

8. What is the most important health problem or health issue today?

9. Do you trust doctors completely? Why or why not?

10. People live longer today than they did 100 years ago. Do you think older people are happier today than they were in the past?

SPEAKING ACTIVITY 6

The teacher will divide the class into four groups. Each group will select either the FOR or the AGAINST statements. The teacher will choose two groups (one for and one against) to debate. Each group will make the arguments listed, support them, and add to them.

Each time one side presents an argument, the other side has the opportunity to respond to the argument until the teams have no more arguments to make. The two groups which did not debate will vote on

which team won the debate. The second two groups will then debate and repeat the process.

Debate topic:

People are better off today than they were 100 years ago.

FOR Statements

  a. People today live longer.

  b. People today have more health care, more doctors, and more hospitals.

  c. We know more about disease and the body.

  d. We have better and more kinds of medicines.

  e. There is a greater variety of food available and it is easier to get food today.

  f. Science has made our lives easier. For example, we have jet planes, big-screen TVs, computers, and all kinds of technology and appliances.

  g. Transportation is better today, including cars, subways, and buses.

  h. Communications are much better, including cellphones and the Internet.

  i. People have more entertainment options available today, including movies, videos, sports, plays, and concerts.

  j. Roads, dams, and buildings are much better today because of modern technology and techniques.

AGAINST Statements

  a. People may live longer, but they don't feel they have a purpose in life. Fewer people are religious or have life goals.

  b. There seems to be more disease than before; for example, there are more cases of cancer, Alzheimer's, allergies, etc.

  c. There are many diseases for which there are no cures. New viruses and other diseases have appeared in the past 100 years.

  d. Many people in the world cannot afford the fancy new medications.

  e. A lot of the food we buy has artificial colour and flavour added, or is genetically modified. It can cause illnesses.

  f. Many people cannot afford the latest gadgets. The latest gadgets also quickly break down and need to be replaced, which creates more garbage.

  g. Cars and buses are contributing to the pollution of the natural environment.

  h. Better communication has made it easier for people to be cheated by criminals.

  i. Much entertainment is violent and geared to the lowest common denominator—the bored and under-educated.

  j. People cut down forests and change the course of rivers and this destroys the natural environment.

PRONUNCIATION

Pronunciation Focus: Stressed and Unstressed Words

Rhythm is made up of the stressed and unstressed words and syllables in English sentences. There are two main rules to keep in mind.

1. In normal fast speech, English speakers usually stress the following kinds of words:

Nouns	food	class	book
Verbs	grow	get	buy
Adjectives	good	nice	cheap
Adverbs	very	fast	hard
Negatives	don't	can't	
Wh- question words	where	how	why
Demonstratives	this/that	these/those	

These are called content words because they carry the meaning of the sentence.

2. English speakers do not usually stress the other kinds of words such as the ones in the following list. These are the words which tell us about the grammatical relations in the sentence. We call these function words.

Personal pronouns	he	him	she	her	they	them	we
Possessive adjectives	his	her	their	our	your	my	
Articles	a	the					
Short prepositions	for	to	of				
Conjunctions	and	or	but	because	when	if	
Auxiliary verbs	did/do	have/has	can/will				
Relative pronouns	who/whom	which	that				

PRONUNCIATION ACTIVITY 1

A. Listen and underline the stressed words in these sentences.    **Track 46**

1. Birds look for worms.
2. The birds are looking for the worms.
3. Don't eat apples.
4. We don't eat the apples.
5. Buy books.
6. I'll buy the books.

7. Learn new words.

8. I'm learning the new words.

9. George does special exercises.

10. George has been doing the special exercises.

B. Each pair of sentences has the same number of stressed syllables and it should take about the same time to say both sentences regardless of the number of words there are in them. In English, speakers give equal time to the number of stresses, not syllables in a sentence. English is a stress-timed language.

C. Practise saying the sentences with a partner.

PRONUNCIATION ACTIVITY 2

A. Limericks are rhyming poems that are often written for children. They are fun to use to practise stressed and unstressed words. Listen to the following limerick.

> There was a young lady whose chin
>
> Resembled the point of a pin.
>
> So she had it made sharp,
>
> And purchased a harp,
>
> And played many tunes with her chin.

B. Now listen to the limerick again and underline the stressed words.

C. Practise saying the limerick with your partner.

PRONUNCIATION ACTIVITY 3

A. Listen to this limerick, and underline the stressed words.

> There was an old man with a beard,
>
> Who said, "It is just as I feared!—
>
> Two owls and a hen,
>
> Four larks and a wren,
>
> Have all built their nests in my beard!"

B. Practise saying this limerick with a partner. Then write a limerick with your partner and teach it to another pair of students.

PRONUNCIATION ACTIVITY 4

Track 49

A. Listen to each sentence and repeat it.

1. I'm sorry you're sick.

2. Can I talk to you now?

3. Thank you for helping.

4. She can do it alone.

5. Where did he go?

6. What can I do?

7. I'd like her to help us move.

8. What's the number of the store?

9. Where did you leave the package?

10. How long do I have to finish the test?

11. Can I get you coffee or tea?

12. We are going to walk to the store.

B. Work with a partner. One partner will say the above sentences while the other listens. Did your partner stress the right words? Now change places.

PRONUNCIATION ACTIVITY 5

A. Listen to each sentence and write the word that is missing on the blank space provided.   **Track 50**

1. She's going _____ the door.

2. It's really up _____ them.

3. What's _____ supper?

4. I'll have _____ see.

5. It's three hundred _____ thirty.

6. It's either thirteen _____ thirty.

7. Can you go _____ see who's at the door?

8. They're brother _____ sister.

9. They're three _____ a quarter.

10. Do you have a lot _____ do?

11. This party is _____ husbands _____ wives.

12. Please wait _____ us.

B. Practise saying the sentences above with a partner.

PRONUNCIATION ACTIVITY 6

A. There are many words in English which are joined by the word *and*. Listen to these food-related expressions and fill in the missing words.   **Track 51**

cream _____ _____   cheese _____ _____

sweet _____ _____   bacon _____ _____

knives _____ _____   meat _____ _____

ham _____ _____   salt _____ _____

cups _____ _____   milk _____ _____

peanut butter _____ _____   surf _____ _____

bread _____ _____   fish _____ _____

B. Listen again and repeat the expressions after the speaker.

PRONUNCIATION ACTIVITY 7

Track 52

A. Listen to these additional expressions joined by the word *and*, and fill in the missing words.

war _____ _____   aches _____ _____

back _____ _____   rights _____ _____

men _____ _____   trial _____ _____

husbands _____ _____   pros _____ _____

brothers _____ _____   neat _____ _____

uncles _____ _____   sick _____ _____

B. Listen again and repeat each expression after the speaker.

C. Work with a partner. Practise saying the expressions to each other. Remember to reduce *and*. Make up a dialogue using as many of these expressions as you can.

PRONUNCIATION ACTIVITY 8

Track 53

A. Listen to each phrase or sentence and circle the words which are stressed, or pronounced clearly.

a (loaf) of (bread)   a cup of coffee

a bunch of flowers   an elephant

a gift for you   on the floor

go to work   Where do you live?

at school   What did he do?

cat and mouse game   What kind does she like?

love it or leave it   She should have stayed.

Did you ask him?   He has worked.

Did you tell her?   We had finished.

Did you introduce them?   Can you do it?

Do you like it?

B. Work with a partner. What is the sound of the words which are not stressed?

C. Practise saying these sentences and phrases to your partner.

PRONUNCIATION ACTIVITY 9

Track 54

A. Listen to these sentences. Write the words that you hear in the blank spaces provided.

1. He's never practised _____ his _____ singing.

2. When _____ it be ready?

3. When _____ moving _____ country?

4. Have _____ introduced _____ each other?

5. Has _____ mother told _____ story?

6. That's what _____ did.

7. I told _____ get ready.

8. We showed _____ store.

9. _____ had a bad experience.

10. _____ know _____?

11. _____ I try _____ help _____?

12. _____ do _____ a favour?

B. When you have finished, check your answers and then practise saying the sentences with a partner.

PRONUNCIATION ACTIVITY 10

A. Listen to the sentences and write what you hear. Then listen again and check your answers. 🎧 **Track 55**

1. _____
2. _____
3. _____
4. _____
5. _____
6. _____
7. _____
8. _____
9. _____
10. _____
11. _____

B. Check your answers with a partner and then with the teacher.

C. With your partner, make up a dialogue using as many of the phrases as you can.

COMMUNICATING IN THE REAL WORLD

Use your English to talk to people outside your classroom. On your own or with a partner, talk to five people outside your class. Make up your own questions based on the topics in this chapter or ask the questions below and record the information.

Make a short report to the class about what you learned.

Here is one way to introduce your assignment.

> Could I ask you some questions? I am doing an assignment for my English class.

1. What is the most unusual food you have ever eaten?
2. What foods are you crazy about?
3. What foods can't you stand?
4. What's your opinion of exercise?
5. How much physical activity do you think adults need?
6. Why do you think women live longer than men?
7. What is the most important health problem or health issue today?

SELF-EVALUATION

Think about your work in this chapter. For each row in the chart sections **Grammar and Language Functions**, **Learning Strategies**, and **Pronunciation**, give yourself a score based on the rating scale below and write a comment in the Notes section.

Show the chart to your teacher. Talk about what you need to do to make your English better.

Rating Scale

| 1 | 2 | 3 | 4 | 5 |

Needs improvement. ←————————————————————→ *Great!*

	Score	Notes
Grammar and Language Functions		
talking about events in the indefinite past using the present perfect tense		
expressing likes and dislikes		
stating opinions		
agreeing and disagreeing with others' opinions		
supporting opinions		
Pronunciation		
understanding and pronouncing stressed and unstressed words in English sentences and phrases correctly		

Learning Strategies

Speaking

using complete sentences when I ask or answer questions to help me develop fluency		
when I am answering questions, checking to see if the listener understands		
encouraging myself by reminding myself that I am just as good as others at getting my message across		

Listening

listening for definitions or explanations to help me understand new or difficult words		
as I listen, formulating questions about points that are not clear to me to help me discuss these points later		

Vocabulary and Language Chunks

Look at this list of new vocabulary and language chunks you learned in this chapter. Give yourself a score based on the rating scale and write a comment.

the sight of	no worries	as simple as that
to break up with	to make up for	to take the stairs
to shy away from	to do something about	that'll do it
high up on the list	on the other hand	at risk of
to warn about	prescription drugs	to stay healthy
likely to	to throw away	in other words
to pass on to someone	to back up	to look into
to pick out	physical activity	to take a walk
to pass up	risk factor	to open up to
to start out		

	Score	Notes
understanding new vocabulary and language chunks		
using new words and phrases correctly		

Write eight sentences and use new vocabulary you learned in this chapter.

1. _____
2. _____
3. _____
4. _____
5. _____
6. _____
7. _____
8. _____

My plan for practising is _____

_____

_____

_____

_____

CHAPTER 5

Thrills and Chills

Leisure, Sports, and Entertainment

Stating and asking about preferences

Expressing ability and inability

Expressing advisability

Regretting, reprimanding, and criticizing

Summarizing

Expressing possibility/speculating

Expressing possibility in the past/speculating about past events

THINKING AND TALKING

You can learn more about a man in one hour of play than in a lifetime of conversation.

—Plato, Greek philosopher

Cultivated leisure is the aim of man.

—Oscar Wilde, British writer

Work in groups and discuss what these quotes mean. Do you agree with them?

What's your own idea of leisure? What do you enjoy doing in your free time?

SPEAKING ACTIVITY 1

Work with a group. In a 2013 poll about favourite leisure activities in the United States, some of the activities in the list below were included. Work with your group to rank the top six activities that you think Americans chose. Give "1" to the most popular activity, "2" to the second-most popular, and so on. Present your ranking to the class. Ask your teacher about the original rankings.

Speaking STRATEGY

When you want to say something, use body language and eye contact to let people know you are ready to speak. You can look at the speaker to let her or him know that you are waiting to speak. You can also lean forward or lean towards the speaker.

travelling	watching TV	using social media
playing music	reading	watching movies
shopping	walking	playing sports
going to the movies	fishing	golfing
gardening	playing computer games	relaxing and thinking
eating out	spending time with pets or animals	hunting
dancing	working on the computer	spending time with family and friends
doing exercise, or other recreational activities		

SPEAKING 1

Communication Focus 1:
Stating and Asking about Preferences

Structures/Expressions	Examples
. . . would rather . . .	He would rather watch TV than go for a walk. Would you rather listen to pop or classical music?
. . . prefer . . .	She prefers dancing to swimming. Do you prefer Indian or Thai food?
I like . . . better than . . .	I like playing baseball better than playing hockey. Which do you like better, going out to a movie or watching it at home?
I don't like . . . as much as . . .	I don't like playing hockey as much as playing baseball.

SPEAKING ACTIVITY 2

Work with a partner. Ask these questions. Report the most interesting answers to the class.

1. Would you rather go to a movie or to a play? Why?
2. Would you rather listen to pop music or to classical music? Why?
3. Would you rather go to a party or go to the museum? Why?
4. Would you rather read a comic book or a novel? Why?
5. Would you rather go to an amusement park or to a shopping mall? Why?
6. Would you rather go skydiving or bungee jumping? Why?
7. Would you rather go to a karaoke bar or to a concert? Why?
8. Would you rather watch a cartoon or a news program? Why?
9. Would you rather have a party or go to a party as a guest? Why?
10. Would you rather go out for dinner or stay home and cook dinner? Why?
11. Which leisure activities do you prefer?
12. Which outdoor activities do you prefer?
13. Which social activities do you prefer?

ᾗᾗᾗ SPEAKING ACTIVITY 3

Work in a group. Make a quick chart with the headings below. Find out the similarities and differences between you and your classmates. Discuss with each other why you prefer these activities to others.

Name	What is your favourite sport?	What is your favourite leisure activity?	What sport or activity do you dream of taking up?

LISTENING 1: EXTREME SPORTS— A RADIO INTERVIEW

Before You Listen

ᾗᾗ Pre-listening Vocabulary

A. You will hear an interview on the audio CD that includes the following vocabulary. Work with a partner or by yourself to write the correct word next to its definition in the chart below.

extreme	risk	individual	overwhelming
diving	enthusiast	focus	thrills
cliff	board	folks	element
challenge	freestyle	to reveal	gear
hype	track	alternative	parachuting
surfing	to appeal		

Definitions	Vocabulary
1. steep rock face	*cliff*
2. a piece of wood used for skiing or skating	
3. jumping from an airplane using a large fabric umbrella-like device to slow down the fall	
4. feelings of great excitement and emotion	
5. a person who is very eager or keen about a hobby	
6. the main point of attention	
7. one person; single	
8. a part of something, a component	
9. another option or possibility	
10. to attract, to interest	

11. excessive, intense, very great	
12. contest; test	
13. riding waves in the ocean using a special board	
14. a lot of publicity, advertising	
15. overpowering, great, huge	
16. jumping into water or through air	
17. equipment	
18. people	
19. pathway, small road, trail	
20. to show	
21. free to choose any style or way	
22. danger, hazard	

B. Choose the correct vocabulary from the list above to fill in the blanks in these sentences. Use each word only once. Not all the words are used in the sentences. Please make changes to verbs or nouns when necessary.

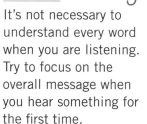

Listening STRATEGY
It's not necessary to understand every word when you are listening. Try to focus on the overall message when you hear something for the first time.

1. A friend of mine went base jumping off a very high ____cliff____ in the Rocky Mountains.

2. The weather is very hot in summer and very cold in winter. The temperatures are not moderate. They are _____.

3. Extreme sports are sports with more adventure and more _____ to personal safety.

4. TV sports stations have to show more _____ or different kinds of sports to keep viewers happy.

5. Fans of extreme sports, or extreme sports _____ are looking for great excitement. They are _____ seekers.

6. Extreme sports _____ to people of all ages.

7. He doesn't follow the regular patterns when bicycling. He prefers doing _____ riding.

8. Base jumping is jumping or _____ off very high structures and buildings.

9. If people engage in extreme sports they need to use all the protective _____ that is necessary.

10. There is a lot of advertising or _____ about extreme sports on all the sports stations.

11. Wind _____ involves standing on a _____ on the surface of the water as the wind pushes you forward.

12. In extreme sports, each person or _____ is competing against himself.

13. Extreme sports can be dangerous, but some people enjoy the _____ of competing against themselves.

 **Pre-listening Activity**

Work with a partner. You are going to listen to an interview about extreme sports. Discuss and list extreme sports that you know about. Then talk about what you want to find out about extreme sports.

Listening for the Main Ideas

 Track 56   Listen to the interview once and answer the questions.

1. What kind of show is this?
2. What is the purpose of this show?
3. Why did the host invite the guest to be on the show?
4. How does the host of the show feel about the topic?

Listening Comprehension

Track 57   Listen to the interview as many times as necessary. As you listen, write down two points that you hear about each of the topics listed.

Extreme sports

1. _____
2. _____

The focus in extreme sports

1. _____
2. _____

Who do extreme sports appeal to?

1. _____
2. _____

BMX

1. _____
2. _____

Skateboarding

1. _____
2. _____

Base jumping

1. _____
2. _____

Zorbing

1. _____
2. _____

Volcano boarding

1. _____

2. _____

Why do people do these extreme sports?

1. _____

2. _____

Personalizing

Work in a group. Decide as a group which two extreme sports you would like to try and which ones you would never try. Present your choices to the class and explain why you have selected each sport.

Listening STRATEGY

Identify and make a list of words that you do not understand and then find out their meanings.

VOCABULARY AND LANGUAGE CHUNKS

Write the number of each expression next to its meaning. After checking your answers, choose six expressions and write your own sentences.

Expressions		Meanings
1. to keep someone up to date	_____	proper, correct conduct, where people are treated fairly and equally
2. old stand-by	_____	to do as well as you can
3. to do your best	_____	to participate
4. to take one's breath away	_____	to spread through the world
5. to come to mind	_____	to do something; to try for something
6. to sweep the world	_1_	to provide the latest information to someone
7. to go for it	_____	to get excited and lose control
8. to take part in	_____	to cause someone to be out of breath due to shock, hard exercise, or excitement
9. fair play	_____	old favourite; something people rely on and use often
10. to get carried away	_____	to appear in thoughts, in the mind

SPEAKING ACTIVITY 4

A. Work in a group. Choose three sports from the list on the next page for each category. Put them in order (for example, give "1" to the most dangerous activity, "2" to the second-most dangerous, and so on). You can add others to the list also.

Speaking STRATEGY

When you are ready to speak, let the others know by making polite sounds such as *ah*, *um*, *okay*, or *I think* . . . to signal that you are ready to speak.

tobogganing	boxing	skydiving	wrestling
volcano boarding	cycling	hockey	canoeing
football	karate	golf	skateboarding
water skiing	skiing	basketball	baseball
auto racing	soccer	swimming	fishing
zorbing	Ping-Pong	yoga	volleyball
base jumping	windsurfing	bowling	billiards
scuba diving	jogging	weightlifting	

The most dangerous sport	1.	2.	3.
The most exciting sport	1.	2.	3.
The most relaxing sport	1.	2.	3.
The most fun	1.	2.	3.

B. When you have finished, think up your own categories for the sports in the list. The group which comes up with the most categories is the winner.

SPEAKING 2

Communication Focus 2: Expressing Ability and Inability

To express ability we use *can*, *could*, or *to be able to*.

Affirmative	Negative	Interrogative
Present		
I can swim very well.	He can't run.	Can you windsurf?
I am able to swim very well.	He isn't able to run.	Are you able to windsurf?
Past		
I could swim very well when I was a child.	He couldn't run very fast last week.	Could you windsurf when you were at the beach?
I was able to swim very well after I took lessons.	He wasn't able to run after he hurt his ankle.	Were you able to windsurf last summer?
Future		
I will be able to swim next week.	He won't be able to run after his operation.	Will you be able to windsurf next summer?

Grammar Note: The Meanings of *could* and *was/were able to*

Can/could and *to be able to* all express ability. The meanings are the same, except in the past tense. In the past, *could* means past ability only. *Was/were able to* has the meaning of past ability and accomplishment.
Examples:

> As a teenager, my brother could run very fast. He was able to win the marathon.

> Barbara was able to win the gold medal at the Olympics because she could skate very well.

SPEAKING ACTIVITY 5

Work with a partner. Begin by making a three-column list on your own with the headings **Five to Ten Years Ago**, **Present Time**, and **In the Future**. List all the activities and sports that you were able to do five to ten years ago, those you can do at the present time, and those you hope to be able to do in the future. Compare lists with your partner and discuss the similarities and differences.

Speaking STRATEGY

Don't be afraid to try anything to get your message across. You can use pictures, gestures, spelling, or anything else that helps you.

Communication Focus 3: Expressing Advisability

We often use *should* to express advisability in the present and future.

Affirmative	Negative	Interrogative
You should exercise more.	He shouldn't eat a heavy meal before swimming.	Should I join a health club?

Other Structures/Expressions to Express Advisability	Examples
It's a good idea . . .	It's a good idea to wear a helmet if you are cycling.
It's advisable . . .	It's advisable to wear knee pads when you are learning to skateboard.
. . . had better . . .*	You had better learn the vocabulary or else you will fail.
. . . ought to . . .**	You ought to stretch before running.

*. . . *had better* is very strong. We often use *had better . . . or else* to warn people.
Ought to* has the same meaning as *should* **but is not usually used in negatives or questions.

Should is a very strong way to express advisability. We don't use *should* when making suggestions to peers or people of higher status. A coach might use *should* with a trainee, a teacher might use *should* when speaking to a student, or a doctor might use *should* when speaking to a patient.

Expressing Regret

State what really happened in the examples below.
Examples:

> I shouldn't have spent all my money on clothes.
>
> I should have started studying for the test earlier.

Reprimanding

State what really happened in the examples below.
Examples:

> You shouldn't have driven so fast.
>
> You should have been polite to the police officer.

Criticizing

State what really happened in the examples below.
Examples:

> The students shouldn't have cheated. It was wrong.
>
> Allan should have left the server a bigger tip. He's so cheap!

SPEAKING ACTIVITY 8

Work with a partner. You will ask each other about some regrets you have about the past by asking and answering the following questions. Use *should* (or *shouldn't have*) + the past participle.

1. What regrets do you have about your education?
2. What regrets do you have about your personal life?
3. What regrets do you have about your family?
4. What do you regret about something you did recently?
5. What do you regret about something you didn't do?

LISTENING 2: IS VIOLENT MEDIA JUST ENTERTAINMENT?—A LECTURE

Before You Listen

Pre-listening Vocabulary

A. You will hear a lecture on the audio CD that includes the vocabulary at the top of the next page. Work with a partner or by yourself to write the correct word next to its definition in the chart that follows.

to condense	to assassinate	to increase	to survey
death	comprehensive	to decrease	randomly
to quadruple	research	numb	empathy
blast	participants	suffering	correlation
megaton	to deny	physiological arousal	violence
to skip	die		to stab
graphic			

Definitions	Vocabulary
1. to make shorter or smaller by taking less important parts out	*to condense*
2. people who take part in something	
3. act of dying	
4. ability to understand and share other people's feelings	
5. to refuse to agree; to say something is not true	
6. use of force to hurt or destroy; strong, powerful actions	
7. to become four times as big; to multiply by four	
8. sudden and violent explosion	
9. strong physical or bodily response; a waking up	
10. one million tons of explosion power	
11. to become larger or greater in size	
12. to leave out; to omit	
13. to become smaller or less in size or number	
14. giving a clear picture; describing in detail	
15. a relationship or connection between two or more things, often used in research and studies	
16. to kill; to murder, suddenly and secretively	
17. not able to feel anything	
18. feeling pain and extreme distress	
19. complete, including everything	
20. careful study to find and report new information	
21. singular form of the word *dice*	
22. to examine, to look over	
23. with no particular pattern, order, or purpose	
24. to pierce or wound with a knife or sharp object	

B. Choose the correct vocabulary from the list above to fill in the blanks in these sentences. Use each word only once. Not all the words are used in the sentences. Please make changes to verbs or nouns when necessary.

1. The lecturer ____condensed____ the results of all the studies for the students.

2. The number of crimes increased four times. The number _____.

3. The loud noise or _____ of the explosion frightened all the people.

4. That movie is restricted to people over 18 years of age because of all the _____ in it.

5. In the movie *Psycho*, the killer _____ the victim to _____ with a knife.

6. In some video games players can kill or _____ famous people like John Kennedy.

7. It's important for people to have _____ or sympathetic feelings towards others, to try to understand what they are feeling and to put themselves in others' shoes.

8. He didn't read the second chapter of the book. He _____ it.

9. Playing violent video games can _____ angry feelings.

10. Video games can make people _____ or unable to feel the pain and _____ of other people.

11. In the study, they assigned people to play violent or non-violent video games _____ or not in any specific order.

12. They asked the people involved or the _____ in the study to complete a story.

13. He said he didn't commit the crime. He _____ it.

14. When people in the study stopped playing violent games their angry behaviour _____.

15. He wanted to do studies or _____ about what effects violent video games have on players.

👥 Pre-listening Activity

A. Work with a partner. What are the two most popular video games today? How would you describe them? What were video games like 15 years ago? Compare and contrast the most popular video games people play today with video games people used to play 15 years ago.

B. Work with a partner to discuss the following.

1. Describe a movie or TV show with violence in it that you saw recently.

2. Describe a violent video game that you have played or have heard about.

3. What is the reason for the violence? In your opinion, is the violence necessary? Why?

4. How do you think violence in movies and video games influences people?

C. In the lecture you are going to hear, Brad Bushman talks about how violence has increased in media and movies. He gives the example of an old movie, *Psycho*, (he calls it "Psycho 1") which would be many times more violent if it were made today. He talks about the chart below. Discuss what you think this chart shows and predict what you think the lecturer will say. Join another pair of students and compare your predictions.

Violent Video Game Effects

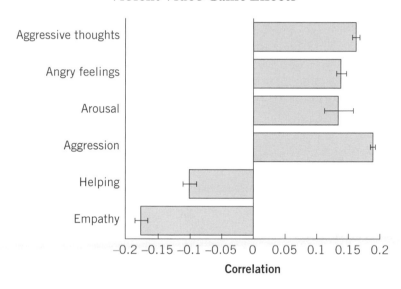

Correlation

Listening STRATEGY

If you can connect the information that you hear in a listening to your own knowledge, experiences, and opinions, you will have a deeper understanding of the information and will be able to evaluate it better.

Listening for the Main Ideas

Listen to the lecture once, and then answer the three questions.

🎧 **Track 58**

1. What is the purpose of the lecture?
2. What main points does the speaker make?
3. What are the lecturer's feelings and opinions about the topic?

Listening Comprehension

You are going to take notes. One way to take notes is to write down details that you hear about a topic or main idea. The main topics in the lecture have been written down for you. Write notes about some of the details. The details for the first two topics have already been done for you as an example.

🎧 **Track 59**

Listen to the lecture again and fill in the blanks with the details. You may listen to the lecture as many times as necessary.

Lecture Notes Part 1

SPEAKER'S BACKGROUND

Brad Bushman

- _doing research_ on violent _media_ over _25_ years

- difficult to condense _25_ years research into _45_ minutes

OPENING QUOTATION

- director of _All the President's Men_

- "Movie violence is like _eating salt_. The more you eat, the more _you need_ to eat _to taste_ it. That's why _death_ counts have _quadrupled_ and blast power is increasing by _"the megaton."_"

EXAMPLE OF INCREASING VIOLENCE

Movie "Psycho 1"

A man _____ with a _____ while she's taking a shower.

Prediction for movie "Psycho 3"

_____ the _____. Bring in the _____.

CONCLUSION ABOUT VIOLENCE

The media is becoming _____.

Lecture Notes Part 2

What main topics is the lecturer going to talk about? Check all that apply.

1. Violent video games' effects
2. Why people deny media effects
3. Positive media effects
4. Television programs and movies

REVIEW OF STUDIES

Number of studies: _____

Number of participants: _____

Where the studies were done: _____

Who participated: _____

What does a correlation of zero mean? _____

Size of effects on chart: _____

RESULTS OF STUDIES

Effects of playing violent video games:

1. _____

2. _____

3. _____

4. _____

5. _____

6. _____

AGGRESSIVE THOUGHTS STUDY

Method

1. _____

2. _____

PARTICIPANTS READ THIS STORY STEM AND COMPLETE IT.

1. Todd's on his way home from work.

2. _____

3. _____

4. He walks over to the other car.

5. What happens next?

_____

WHY DO THE GAME PLAYERS HAVE TO COMPLETE THIS STORY STEM?

_____

_____

FILL IN THE PERCENTAGES IN THE CHART BELOW.

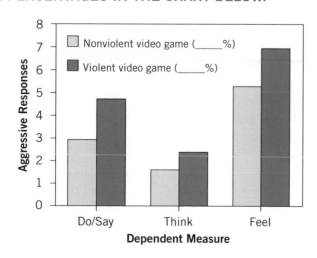

CONCLUSION OF THE AGGRESSIVE THOUGHTS STUDY

_____

Personalizing

A. Work in a group. As a group, what is your opinion about each of the following topics? What are your reasons? Decide if there should be some control of what we see in entertainment and who should control it.

Topic	My Opinion	Group Opinion and Support
Violence in TV shows		
Violence in movies		
Violence in music and music videos		
Violence in video games		
Violence on the Internet		

B. Work with a partner and answer these questions. Report to the class.
1. What do people learn from playing video games?
2. Why should we or shouldn't we let children play video games?
3. Do you believe video games can make people aggressive and violent? Why or why not?
4. What benefits are there to playing video games?
5. What do you think video games will be like in the future?

VOCABULARY AND LANGUAGE CHUNKS

Write the number of each expression next to its meaning. After checking your answers, choose six expressions and write your own sentences.

Expressions	Meanings
1. margin of error	__1__ an extra amount allowed because there might be a mistake in calculations; percentage of mistakes possible

2. to conduct a study   _____   to drive through a red or yellow traffic light

3. statistically significant   _____   to get injured

4. to be stressed out   _____   to explain or show something to someone

5. to make sure   _____   along one's route

6. to roll a die   _____   to hit someone with the fists repeatedly

7. in fact   _____   to kick someone's behind

8. to kick out something   _____   actually, in reality, in truth

9. to kick someone's butt*   _____   to break something by kicking

10. to throw punches   _____   to throw one of a pair of dice

11. on one's way   _____   to check, to make certain

12. to take someone through   _____   to be tense, nervous, and anxious

13. to get hurt   _____   result which is not accidental, which means one thing is related to another in a study

14. to run the light   _____   to organize and do research

*rude expression only used in very casual speech

Communication Focus 5: Summarizing

We summarize when we relate the highlights or main points of longer written or spoken texts such as articles, stories, or reports.

Structures/Expressions	Examples
The main points are . . .	The main points are that there has been an increase in violence in the media and that this has a negative effect on society.
The most important issues are . . .	The most important issues are the violence in video games and its effect on game players.
In summary, . . .	In summary, the lecturer believes that violent video games cause people to have angry aggressive thoughts.
To conclude, . . .	To conclude, he feels that violent video games increase aggressive thoughts and behaviour.
In a nutshell, . . .	In a nutshell, he believes media violence has a very negative effect on society.

SPEAKING ACTIVITY 9

Work with a partner. Discuss your feelings and ideas about the following topics. Then summarize your discussions for the class.

Topics	Main Points
Violence in society	
War	
Terrorism	
Crime on the Internet	
Censorship	
Freedom of speech	
Children's rights	
Individual rights	
Women's rights	
The inequality of rich people and poor people in society	
Native peoples' rights	

Communication Focus 6: Expressing Possibility/Speculating

When we want to say there is a 50 percent chance of something being true in the present or in the future, we use *might*, *may*, or *could*:

Affirmative	Negative	Interrogative
The pictures **might frighten** the child.	The pictures **might not frighten** the child. (He might not be afraid.)	**Might** the pictures **frighten** the child?*
The story **could upset** her.		**Could** the story **upset** her?
The program **may scare** them.	The program **may not scare** them. (They may laugh at it.)	

*Using *might* to ask *Yes/No* questions is formal sounding and is not often used.

We can also use these expressions:

It's possible . . .	**It's possible that the pictures will frighten the child.**
Perhaps . . .	**Perhaps the story will upset her.**
Maybe . . .	**Maybe the program will scare them.**

SPEAKING ACTIVITY 10

Work with a partner. What changes do you think might take place in the next 20 years? What could happen in the areas listed below? When you have finished, join another pair of students. Compare your ideas. What similarities and differences did you find? Summarize your discussions for the class.

Topics	What changes do you think we might see in 20 years?
TV	
Music	
Video games	
Internet	
Websites	
Movies	
Cars	
Planes	
Education	
Children	
Men	
Women	
This country	
Other:	

SPEAKING ACTIVITY 11

Work with a partner. Talk about where you each might be and what you might do 10 years from now. Once you have finished, make a quick chart with the headings shown below. Speculate about three of your classmates and write down your predictions in the chart. Show your ideas to these classmates. Find out if anyone had any ideas about you. Report the most interesting predictions to the class.

Name	Place	Activities

Communication Focus 7: Expressing Possibility in the Past/Speculating about Past Events

When we want to say that there is a 50 percent chance that something was true in the past, we use *might have*, *may have*, or *could have*:

Affirmative	Negative	Interrogative
They **might have gone** to the party.	They **might not have gone** to the party.	**Might** they **have gone** to the party?*
They **could have returned** to the hotel.		**Could** they **have returned** to the hotel?
They **may have learned** to play that video game.	They **may not have learned** to play that video game.	

*We don't usually use *might have* in asking *Yes/No* questions. It is too formal sounding.

SPEAKING ACTIVITY 12

Work with a partner to speculate about what might have happened in the following mysterious situations. When you have finished, join another pair of students and share your answers.

Topic	What might have happened? What could have happened? What may have happened?
Why did the dinosaurs disappear?	
What happened to Atlantis?	
How did the ancient Egyptians build huge structures like the pyramids?	
Who invented writing?	
Why did the Neanderthals disappear?	
How did humans discover fire?	
How did human language start?	
What happened to the Mayan civilization?	
Who built Stonehenge?	
Who put up all the statues on Easter Island?	
Your mystery:	

PRONUNCIATION

Pronunciation Focus:
Linking Words in Connected Speech

In normal fast speech in English, words can be joined over word boundaries. If speakers don't do this, their speech may sound unnatural or may be confusing, or even unintelligible to the listener. We link words under several different conditions.

 Track 60

Condition 1

In English, when a word begins with a vowel and is preceded by a word ending in a consonant, the sound of the consonant is linked to the following vowel. For example, "Pick it up," "Turn it on," and "Hand one over."

 **PRONUNCIATION ACTIVITY 1**

A. Listen to these sentences and phrases and underline the places where the links occur. Check your answers.

a. I got up at eleven.
b. I love it.
c. All washed up.
d. Watch it.
e. March on.
f. Watch out.
g. We are doing it over.
h. Give up.

i. Step over it.
j. Breathe out.
k. Hand out the papers.
l. It's up on the shelf.
m. We found him.
n. That's a lot of oranges.
o. This afternoon at five o'clock.

 Track 61

B. Listen again and repeat each sentence after you hear it.

C. Work with a partner. Say the sentences to each other. Make sure that you are each linking the words together. Choose some sentences from this list and make up a dialogue which you will do for the class.

D. Work with a partner. Look at the phrases below. Predict if and where linking will happen in each phrase. Check your answers with the teacher and then practise saying the phrases.

a. Put it on.
b. Take it off.
c. Eat all the food up.
d. I walked over to the car.
e. It spilled all over us.

f. She got over it.
g. We broke our eggs.
h. He helped her escape.
i. How did you work it out?
j. He couldn't ever figure it out.

Condition 2

 Track 62

When a word ends with one of the consonants *p*, *b*, *t*, *d*, *k*, or *g*, and the next word begins with a consonant, these final consonants are pronounced but not released; that is, they are not strongly pronounced. This means that we hold the final consonant until we are ready to say the next word.

 **PRONUNCIATION ACTIVITY 2**

A. Listen and repeat these phrases.

a. keep going
b. big deal
c. look funny
d. stop sign
e. get caught
f. went down
g. walk tall

h. get thirsty
i. cab driver
j. job seeker
k. sad story
l. mad money
m. big storm
n. cold spell

B. Work with a partner. Say the phrases to each other.

C. Choose some phrases from this list and make up a dialogue which you will do for the class.

Condition 3

When a word begins with the same consonant as the previous word ends with, the consonant is pronounced as one slightly longer sound.

 **Track 63**

 **PRONUNCIATION ACTIVITY 3**

A. Listen and repeat these phrases.

a. slap Peter	f. hide Donna	k. quiz Zena
b. punch Charles	g. hug Gord	l. tap Paul
c. push Sharon	h. grab Barbara	m. both things
d. hit Terry	i. thank Kate	n. bathe them
e. kick Catherine	j. kiss Sue	o. dance steps

B. Work with a partner. Say the phrases to each other.

C. Choose some sentences from this list and make up a dialogue. Present your dialogue to the class.

 **PRONUNCIATION ACTIVITY 4**

A. To practise linking, repeat these phrases.

1. take off your ring	13. tried driving
2. look down	14. tried going
3. look carefree	15. tried on the hat
4. big break	16. got on the bus
5. big gamble	17. got scolded
6. big apple	18. got torn
7. stop it	19. other animals
8. stop people	20. black out
9. help save	21. get over it
10. job search	22. get away with murder
11. job benefits	23. don't put off until tomorrow what you can do today
12. job application	24. get out of our house

Track 64

B. Read the phrases to your partner. Make sure you are linking the words together.

C. With your partner, choose five or more phrases from the list and make up a dialogue. Present your dialogue to the class.

COMMUNICATING IN THE REAL WORLD

Use your English to talk to people outside your classroom. On your own or with a partner, talk to five people outside your class. Make up your own questions based on the topics in this chapter or ask the questions below and record the information.

Make a short report to the class about what you learned.

Here is one way to introduce your assignment.

> Could I ask you some questions? I am doing an assignment for my English class.

1. What is your favourite sport or leisure activity? Why do you like it?
2. Would you rather go out to eat in a restaurant or cook dinner at home? Why?
3. What do you think is a serious problem today and what should we do about it?
4. What's your opinion about violence in the media, in movies, in video games, and on the Internet?
5. What regrets do you have about things you did or didn't do?
6. How do you think humans first discovered language?

SELF-EVALUATION

Think about your work in this chapter. For each row in the chart sections **Grammar and Language Functions**, **Learning Strategies**, and **Pronunciation**, give yourself a score based on the rating scale below and write a comment in the Notes section.

Show the chart to your teacher. Talk about what you need to do to make your English better.

Rating Scale

1	2	3	4	5

Needs improvement. ⟵⟶ *Great!*

	Score	Notes
Grammar and Language Functions		
stating preferences and asking others about their preferences		
expressing ability and inability		
expressing advisability and inadvisability		
regretting, reprimanding, and criticizing		
summarizing the main points		
expressing possibility and speculating		
expressing possibility in the past and speculating about past events		
Pronunciation		
understanding and producing linked words in connected speech		
Learning Strategies		
Speaking		
using body language and eye contact to let people know when I am ready to speak		
letting the others in a conversation know when I am ready to speak by making polite appropriate sounds to signal this.		
using pictures, gestures, spelling, or anything else necessary to help get my message across		
Listening		
focusing on the overall meaning when I hear something for the first time, knowing that I don't have to understand every word when I am listening		
identifying and making lists of words that I don't understand and then finding the meanings		
connecting the information that I hear in a listening to my own knowledge, experiences, and opinions		

Vocabulary and Language Chunks
Look at this list of new vocabulary and language chunks you learned in this chapter. Give yourself a score based on the rating scale and write a comment.

to keep someone up to date	to take part in	to make sure	to take someone through
old stand-by	fair play	to roll a die	to get hurt
to do your best	to get carried away	in fact	to run the light
to take one's breath away	margin of error	to kick out something	on one's way
to come to mind	to conduct a study	to kick someone's butt	to be stressed out
to sweep the world	to go for it	statistically significant	to throw punches

	Score	Notes
understanding new vocabulary and language chunks		
using new words and phrases correctly		

Write eight sentences and use new vocabulary you learned in this chapter.

1. _____
2. _____
3. _____
4. _____
5. _____
6. _____
7. _____
8. _____

My plan for practising is _____

_____

_____

_____

_____

CHAPTER 6

Listening to Your Head and Your Heart

Emotions and Work

Expressing assumptions and probability

Expressing assumptions and probability in the past

Expressing emotions

Making and responding to suggestions

Apologizing and responding

Giving complex descriptions

Adding information and ideas to maintain conversation

Describing skills, knowledge, and abilities

Interrupting

THINKING AND TALKING

What emotions do you think the people in the pictures might be feeling?

A. Work with a group. What do these quotations about emotions mean? Do you agree with them? Why or why not?

> When dealing with people, remember you are not dealing with creatures of logic, but creatures of emotion.
>
> —Dale Carnegie, American writer

> Take control of your . . . emotions and begin to consciously and deliberately reshape your daily experience of life.
>
> —Tony Robbins, motivational speaker

👥 SPEAKING ACTIVITY 1

A. Work with a small group. Brainstorm all the words dealing with emotions that you can think of.

B. Put these emotion words into categories. Try to come up with two or more different categories. You could use categories such as positive/negative, helpful/harmful, and any others you can think of.

👥 SPEAKING ACTIVITY 2

Work with a partner and interview him or her. Report the most interesting information to the class.

1. Are you an emotional person? When and where do you become emotional?
2. Do you think women are more emotional than men? Why or why not?
3. In your day-to-day activities, is it your head (your mind) or your heart (your emotions and feelings) that guides you to make decisions?
4. What do you think the strongest emotions are?
5. In what situations do you think it is important to control your emotions?

Speaking STRATEGY 💬

Use attending behaviours such as looking the speaker in the eye, smiling, nodding, and saying *um*, *uh-uh*, *ah*, *I see*, and *really*. This lets the listener know that you are paying attention, and that you are supportive. This encourages conversation.

6. Do people in your country express their emotions more than people in North America? Give some examples.

7. Would you rather fall in love with an emotional person or a rational person? Why?

8. What was the best emotional experience of your life?

9. Describe a situation when you felt proud of yourself.

10. Describe a situation when you felt afraid.

11. Have you ever felt jealous? When and why?

12. Do you ever feel guilty? When and why?

LISTENING 1: SOCIAL INTELLIGENCE AND LEADERSHIP—AN INTERVIEW

Before You Listen

Pre-listening Vocabulary

A. You will hear an interview on the audio CD that includes the following vocabulary. Work with a partner or by yourself to write the correct word next to its definition in the chart below.

motivation	to face	psychologist	expertise
to handle	aware	passions	grumblings
to interact	insight	executive	mastery
to defer	integration	coaching	to persuade
efforts	discipline	leadership	to inspire

Definitions	Vocabulary
1. a very strong desire to reach a goal or to satisfy a need; the power to start actions	*motivation*
2. expert skill or knowledge in a particular area	
3. to manage	
4. knowing that something (a situation or a problem) exists	
5. deep understanding of a person or situation	
6. very strong emotions which are not easy to control	
7. someone who manages or directs others in a company; someone with high administrative power	
8. to feel you need to give more weight or importance to another person's opinions or ideas than to your own	
9. the act or process of bringing parts together into a whole	

continued on next page

Definitions	Vocabulary
10. a training or development process in which a person is helped to learn certain skills	
11. complete knowledge or skill in something	
12. the ability to be a leader; the personal characteristics to be able to lead	
13. to make someone want to do something; to give someone an idea about what to create	
14. to stand with the face forward; to recognize and deal with; to confront	
15. a specialist in the science of the mind or mental health	
16. training or control requiring rules to be obeyed	
17. expressions of complaint and unhappiness	
18. to cause, influence, or convince someone to do something	
19. work done by mind or body; energy used to do something	
20. to talk to and to do things with others	

B. Choose the correct vocabulary from the list above to fill in the blanks in these sentences. Use each word only once. Not all the words are used in the sentences. Please make changes to verbs or nouns when necessary.

1. People who have emotional intelligence have very strong _____motivation_____ to reach their goals.

2. At work most employees think it is important to _____ to the boss.

3. People who have emotional intelligence are able _____ their emotions and feelings.

4. Empathy is recognizing other people's feelings, knowing how they see things, and using this information _____ or work with them.

5. When there are a lot of _____ or complaints, the boss knows that people are unhappy and that things are not going well.

6. Dan Goleman is a _____ who has a lot of _____ into how people act in the world of work.

7. Dan Goleman has a lot of _____ in social and emotional intelligence.

8. A sign of true _____ is when a manager listens to what workers have to say and uses that information in managing the company.

9. True leaders can convince or _____ and _____ other people.

10. After he received special training or _____ in social intelligence, the manager was able to change and his business performance was much better.

11. Are you _____ of any problems that the employees are complaining about?

👥 Pre-listening Activity 1

Work in a small group. Answer these questions.

Listening STRATEGY

Pay attention to the details to get a clearer picture of the overall message.

1. Which emotions can be beneficial in school or work situations? How?
2. Which emotions can be harmful in school or work situations? How?
3. What is the best way to manage your emotions at school or work?

Listening for the Main Ideas

Listen to the interview once and answer the questions.

🎧 **Track 65**

1. Why is the interviewer interviewing this guest?
2. What topics do they talk about?
3. Who do you think the listeners are?

Listening Comprehension

Listen to the interview again as many times as necessary. As you listen, write the missing information in the outline of the interview.

🎧 **Track 66**

Interviewer: **Diane Coutu**
Interviewer's position:
Guest:
Reason why the guest was invited:
Purpose of the interview:
Definition of emotional intelligence:
Definition of empathy:
Result of guest's work:
Typical example of a problem businesses have:
According to the guest, real leadership is:
Differences between emotional intelligence and social intelligence:

Personalizing

Work with a partner and answer these questions. Summarize your discussion for the class.

1. How much emotional intelligence do you think you have? Rate yourself on a scale of 1 to 5 (1 is the lowest and 5 is the highest). Explain.

2. How important is emotional intelligence in language learning? Explain.

3. How much social intelligence do you think you have? Rate yourself on a scale of 1 to 5 (1 is the lowest and 5 is the highest). Explain.

4. How much of a role do you think social and emotional intelligence play in success in work and in life? Explain.

5. Do you think people can learn emotional and social intelligence? Explain.

6. Describe the occupation you think you would like to have in the future. How important are social and emotional intelligence in this occupation? Explain.

VOCABULARY AND LANGUAGE CHUNKS

Write the number of each expression next to its meaning. After checking your answers, choose six expressions and write your own sentences.

Expressions

1. to be delighted
2. to turn someone on
3. to turn someone off
4. to get in the way
5. to get something done
6. to get better at
7. to turn out
8. to tune in
9. to put something together
10. to have drive

Meanings

__1__ to be very pleased, very happy

_____ to have a strong desire or need to reach a goal

_____ to bring together; to assemble; to integrate

_____ to be attentive to; to pay attention to; to listen to

_____ to become better at; to improve at doing something

_____ to make someone stop paying attention; to make someone lose interest

_____ to make someone feel excited or very interested in something

_____ to interfere with; to prevent something from happening

_____ to accomplish something; to do something

_____ to result; to happen in a particular way

SPEAKING 1

Communication Focus 1:
Expressing Assumptions and Probability

When we make assumptions, we are saying that we are 80 percent or 90 percent sure of something. There are structures for expressing assumptions or probability in the affirmative and the negative, but there is no question form.

Stating Assumptions in the Affirmative

Observations/Facts	Structures/Expressions	Examples
Jake always bites his nails.	*must* + base form of verb *probably*	He **must be** nervous. Jake is **probably** nervous.
Jean and Fred are always together and holding hands.	*must* + base form of verb *probably*	They **must care** about each other. Jean and Fred **probably** care about each other.

Expressing Negative Probability and Assumptions

Observations/Facts	Structures/Expressions	Examples
She never eats pasta.	*can't* + base form of the verb	She **can't like** pasta very much.
	couldn't + base form of the verb	She **couldn't like** pasta very much.
	mustn't + base form of the verb*	She **mustn't like** pasta very much.
	probably not + base form of the verb	She **probably doesn't like** pasta very much.
He works part time.	*can't* + base form of the verb	He **can't make** a lot of money.
	couldn't + base form of the verb	He **couldn't make** a lot of money.
	mustn't + base form of the verb*	He **mustn't make** a lot of money.
	probably not + base form of the verb	He **probably doesn't make** lot of money.

*This is used mostly in spoken English.

🏃 SPEAKING ACTIVITY 3

Work with a partner. Answer these questions using modals of probability.

1. What are people with high levels of social intelligence probably good at?

2. Do you think Dan Goleman has a lot of emotional intelligence? Why or why not?

3. What do you think people in the business world must think about Dan Goleman?

4. What do you think people with a lot of empathy must be good at?

5. What do you think people with high levels of motivation must be like?

6. What do you think an executive's job must be like?

7. What problems do you think emotional people must have? Explain.

8. What do you think psychologists must be good at?

9. How do you think learners must feel when they first start using a new language?

10. How do you think ESL/EFL teachers must feel about their occupation?

11. Do you think top executives have a hard time finding jobs? Why or why not?

12. Do you think psychologists enjoy listening to their patients' problems? Explain.

👥 SPEAKING ACTIVITY 4

A. Work in groups of three. Read the information below about multiple intelligences and then discuss which ones you think you must be strong in and which ones you are probably weak in.

Howard Gardner, a psychologist at Harvard University, used cognitive research to develop a theory that there are many different kinds of intelligences. Gardner thinks of intelligence as the skills and learning styles that enable someone to gain new knowledge and solve problems. He believed people were strong in one or two of these kinds of intelligences, but not in all of them. These are his categories of intelligence.

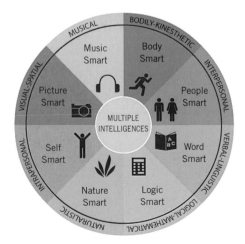

People with **visual–spatial intelligence** are artistic and are aware of their surroundings. They are creative. They like to draw. They visualize pictures and notice colours and shapes. They are good with maps.

People with **bodily–kinesthetic intelligence** use the body effectively. They like movement, making things, and touching people. They communicate well through body language.

People with **musical intelligence** respond to rhythm and sound. They love music. They might study better with music.

People with **interpersonal intelligence** interact very well with others. They learn through interaction. They have many friends, and feel empathy for others.

People with **intrapersonal intelligence** understand themselves and their goals. They're in tune with their inner feelings.

People with **linguistic** intelligence use words effectively. They like reading, playing word games, and making up poetry or stories.

People with **logical–mathematical** intelligence are good at reasoning and calculating. They like to experiment, solve puzzles, and ask questions.

Based on Howard Gardner's theory of multiple intelligences.

B. Fill in the chart below for each person in the group, naming two types of intelligence per category. Report to the class.

	Types of Intelligences	
	Strong	**Weak**
Partner #1		
Partner #2		
Partner #3		

SPEAKING ACTIVITY 5

Work with a partner. State one affirmative and one negative assumption about four famous people you have seen in the news, or about four other people. Give reasons for your assumptions.

Communication Focus 2:
Expressing Assumptions and Probability in the Past

When we want to express 80–90 percent certainty in the past, we use the following structures and expressions. As in the present, there are structures for expressing probability in the affirmative and negative, but there is no question form.

Expressing Assumptions or Probability in the Past

Observations/Facts	Structures/Expressions	Examples
Jane and Larry won the ice dancing competition.	*must have* + past participle	They **must have practised** a lot. They **must have been** very good.
Ellen failed the exam.	*couldn't have* + past participle	Ellen **couldn't have studied** very much.
	can't have + past participle	Ellen **can't have studied** very much.
	mustn't have + past participle*	Ellen **mustn't have studied** very much.
Ellen failed the exam.	*probably* + negative	Ellen **probably didn't study** very much.

*used mostly in spoken English

👥 SPEAKING ACTIVITY 6

Work with a partner. Express assumptions in the past about the following famous personalities. Report to the class.

1. Barack Obama (American politician)
2. Michael Jackson (American singer and entertainer)
3. Bill Gates (American entrepreneur and inventor)
4. Lionel Messi (Spanish soccer player)
5. Yao Ming (Chinese basketball player)
6. Céline Dion (Canadian singer and entertainer)
7. Chris Hadfield (Canadian astronaut)
8. Christopher Columbus (Italian explorer)

Communication Focus 3: Expressing Emotions

The following are some expressions for expressing the emotions of fear, worry, anger, love, and joy. Give three sentences for each emotion. These can be about yourself, a classmate, or someone else. Share your sentences with the class.

Fear

Structures/Expressions
Example:

> **My sister is afraid of heights.**

. . . to be afraid of . . . _____

. . . to be frightened of . . . _____

. . . to be scared of . . . _____

. . . to be terrified of . . . _____

Worry

Structures/Expressions
Example:

> I'm worried about the test.

. . . to be worried about . . .   _____

. . . to be nervous about . . .   _____

. . . to be anxious about . . .   _____

. . . to be uneasy about . . .   _____

Anger

Structures/Expressions
Example:

> I'm angry at my roommate because she never cleans up.

. . . to be angry at/about . . .   _____

. . . to be furious at/about . . .   _____

. . . to be annoyed/irritated by . . .   _____

. . . to be frustrated by . . .   _____

Love

Structures/Expressions
Example:

> My mother loves her pets.

. . . to love . . .   _____

. . . to adore . . .   _____

. . . to be fond of . . .   _____

. . . to feel affection for . . .   _____

Joy/Pleasure

Structures/Expressions
Example:

> We are very pleased about having a day off next Monday.

. . . to be happy/pleased about . . .   _____

. . . to be delighted about . . .   _____

. . . to be thrilled about/by . . .   _____

SPEAKING ACTIVITY 7

Work in a group. Each person will choose one of the five questions A to E below and speak first to the others in the group, and then to all the others in the class, asking his/her question. When you are answering questions, use the expressions for expressing emotions.

When everyone has finished, regroup into five large groups, so that all the As, Bs, Cs, Ds, and Es are together. As a group, put together a class profile based on the information that you found out about fears, worries, etc. Create a chart or a graph and choose someone from each group to report to the class.

A. What are you most afraid/frightened of?

B. What are you worried/nervous about?

C. What are you angry/annoyed about?

D. What are you fond of? What do you love?

E. What are you delighted/thrilled about?

SPEAKING ACTIVITY 8

A. A team of market researchers asked 3,000 people in the US: "What are you most afraid of?" They listed the following 14 fears. Work with a partner and rank them. Rank "1" for the most common fear, "2" for the second-most common, and so on. When you have finished, get together with another pair and compare your answers. Report about the differences between you. The teacher will tell you the survey results.

Fears	Rank	Fears	Rank
speaking before a group	_____	driving, riding in a car	_____
insects and bugs	_____	death	_____
darkness	_____	financial problems	_____
elevators	_____	deep water	_____
flying	_____	heights	_____
escalators	_____	dogs	_____
loneliness	_____	sickness	_____

B. What do you think the top 10 fears must be today? Explain the reasons for the differences.

Communication Focus 4:
Making and Responding to Suggestions

Suggestions are less strong and less direct than advice. We make suggestions to friends, colleagues, and others who have told us about a problem. Don't use *should* to make suggestions because it sounds very strong.

Making Suggestions

Structures/Expressions	Examples
Have you thought of . . .	Have you thought of trying to be friendlier?
You might . . .	You might try to be friendlier.
You could . . .	You could try to be friendlier.
Why don't you . . .	Why don't you try to be friendlier?
How about . . . / what about . . .	How about trying to be friendlier?

Responding to Suggestions

Positive Response	Negative Response
You're right. I should try that.	I'm not sure that's a good idea.
You think so? I'll try that. Thanks.	I don't know about that.
I suppose/guess I should . . .	I don't think that will work.

👥 SPEAKING ACTIVITY 9

The following are some problems that people face when learning a new language. Work with a partner. Choose two problems and develop a dialogue for each. Use expressions for making and responding to suggestions. Role-play your best dialogue for the class.

1. I am afraid to speak English on the phone.
2. I am anxious about making mistakes and often I can't say anything at all in English.
3. I am very nervous about speaking to native speakers. I might not understand them and they probably won't understand me.
4. I am scared of looking stupid because I can't say what I mean in English.
5. I am irritated at not having enough words to express my ideas.
6. English grammar drives me crazy! I can never remember the rules when I am speaking!
7. I am frustrated because whenever I try to say something, no one is able to understand me. It must be my pronunciation.
8. I am uneasy when I am listening to someone speak English, because often I can't follow what they are saying.

Communication Focus 5: Apologizing and Responding

Making an Apology

An apology in English can be simple or complex. It can have up to five distinct features. For a minor offence, such as stepping on someone's toe or bumping into someone, we use only an expression of regret. It's not necessary to give an explanation. In other cases, English speakers use an expression of regret and give an explanation. They might also add some other elements depending on how serious the offence is, the relationship of the speakers, and the context.

Features of an Apology	Examples	
1. Expression of regret	I am very/really/awfully sorry. I apologize. I owe you an apology.	Please forgive me. Excuse me* Pardon me*
2. Acknowledgement of responsibility	It's my fault. I broke the glass.	I lost your book.
3. Explanation or account of what happened	The glass slipped. I forgot. My car broke down.	I wasn't thinking. I didn't see you.
4. Offer of repair	Let me get you a new one. Could we reschedule?	How can I make it up to you?
5. Promise of non-recurrence	I'll be more careful next time.	It won't happen again.

*These phrases are used for very minor offences and we don't need to use the other elements of a formal apology with these.

Formal Responses to an Apology

Positive (accepting the apology)	Negative (not accepting the apology)
That's all right.	I'm sorry, an apology isn't enough.
Please don't worry about it.	I don't think I can accept your apology.
I accept your apology.	

Less Formal Responses to an Apology

Positive (accepting the apology)	Negative (not accepting the apology)
You couldn't help it.	It's not okay.
It wasn't your fault.	You did it on purpose.
No problem. No worries!	

🏃 SPEAKING ACTIVITY 10

Work in a small group. Talk about the last time you each apologized. Where were you? What happened? Who did you apologize to? What did you say? What was the response?

Name	Location	Reason for Apology	Who did you apologize to?	What did you say?	Response

🏃 SPEAKING ACTIVITY 11

A. Work with a partner. Choose three situations and role-play apologizing and responding to apologies.

B. Perform one of your role-plays for the class. As you listen to your classmates' role-plays, write down which of the five features of an apology mentioned above are in each role-play.

1. You borrowed your friend's favourite sweater and you can't remember where you left it.

2. You missed a test. You had a terrible migraine headache.

3. You couldn't go out for your friend's birthday because your boyfriend/girlfriend had tickets for a concert on that day.

4. You missed your appointment with the counsellor because you had to take a sick friend to the hospital.

5. You borrowed your friend's laptop and now it has stopped working.

6. You spilled red wine on your teacher's white carpet.

LISTENING 2: AUSTRALIA FLOODED BY DREAM JOB APPLICANTS— A NEWS REPORT

Before You Listen

👥 Pre-listening Vocabulary

A. You will hear a news report on the audio CD that includes the following vocabulary. Work with a partner or by yourself to write the correct word next to its definition in the chart below.

officials	finalist	vacant	outback
funster	posts	to showcase	specific
footage	wildlife	mad	series
standout	VIP	access	exclusive
to top	territory	genuine	competition
global			

Definitions	Vocabulary
1. people employed by a government or organization who are responsible for controlling or regulating activities	*officials*
2. worldwide; of the whole world	
3. particular; clearly identified	
4. some film or video of something	
5. a number of things or events	
6. an area of land, especially in Canada, the US, lor Australia, which is not yet a state or province	
7. actual, real, true	
8. a person who competes in the last part of a competition or contest	
9. not open to everyone; only open to special people	
10. the right or ability to enter or approach	
11. to reach the highest place or number	
12. very important person	
13. a person who performs exceptionally well at something; someone every one notices	

14. empty, unfilled	
15. remote, uninhabited inland part of Australia	
16. a person who creates fun, who tries to amuse others	
17. jobs; positions	
18. crazy, enthusiastic, excited	
19. to show, display, exhibit	
20. animals and creatures living in the wild	
21. contest; the process of trying to win something	

B. Choose the correct vocabulary from the list above to fill in the blanks in these sentences. Use each word only once. Not all the words are used in the sentences. Please make changes to verbs or nouns when necessary.

1. The people in charge of the soccer games during the World Cup are the _____officials_____.

2. Tourists who visit South Africa usually want to see all the _____ on an animal preserve.

3. The actor made a short video because he wanted _____ his acting skills. He sent the _____ to a few directors.

4. The tourism department of Australia is running a _____ to find the best employees.

5. There are several _____ positions in that company that they want to fill.

6. That company has offices all over the world. They are a _____ business.

7. Is that imitation leather or is it _____?

8. Australia is very big. It has a huge _____.

9. They only invite VIPs to their parties. These events are very _____.

10. That company is advertising two jobs in Canada and three more _____ in the US.

11. Please give me some _____ details about the job. I want more than just general information.

12. I don't have a key so I don't have _____ to the office.

👥 Pre-listening Activity 1

Work with a partner. Brainstorm all the words that come to mind under the heading "The Best Jobs in the World."

👥 Pre-listening Activity 2

Work with a partner and look at the pictures below. What country do you think this is? Why? Make a list of five things you know about this country. Then make a list of jobs that might be popular there. Use the headings **What We Know** and **Popular Jobs**.

Listening for the Main Ideas

🎧 Track 67

Listen to the report once and answer the questions.

1. What is this report about?
2. Why is this story on the news?
3. How does the reporter feel about the subject of the news report?

Listening Comprehension

🎧 Track 68

Listen to the report as many times as necessary. Write *T* if the statement is true or *F* if it is false.

Listening STRATEGY 👂

Try to identify key words, which are the important words often repeated throughout a text. This will help you understand what the listening is about.

1. Australian tourists apply for the best jobs in the world. __False__
2. This competition to find six employees is global. _____
3. The six people who are chosen will work for 18 months. _____
4. There are hundreds of applications from all over the world. _____
5. Officials have to choose 18 finalists for each job. _____
6. Sixty thousand people from 200 countries have applied for these jobs. _____
7. The salary for each job is about 10,000 US dollars. _____
8. Each applicant submitted a 30-minute video of their skills. _____
9. One official says it's going to be easy to choose the finalists. _____
10. The finalists have to fly to Australia for interviews. _____
11. The finalists will participate in events in different cities and states. _____

12. The job of funster involves going to parties and festivals in Sydney. _____

13. The job of outback adventurer will include living in the Australian bush. _____

14. The taste master will write about food and drink in Australia. _____

15. The highest number of applications came from Europe. _____

Personalizing

Work with a partner. Ask and answer the following questions. Report the most interesting answers to the class.

1. Which of the three jobs mentioned in this report would you like to have? Explain why.
2. Why do you think Australia has this kind of contest?
3. What is your dream job? How do you think you could achieve that dream?

Listening STRATEGY
If you evaluate your ability to follow the main ideas and details, you will be better able to manage your problem areas in listening.

VOCABULARY AND LANGUAGE CHUNKS

Write the number of each expression next to its meaning. After checking your answers, choose six expressions and write your own sentences.

Expressions	Meanings
1. to hold a competition	__1__ to organize a contest
2. to face a task	_____ from every country in the world
3. to pull something together	_____ to experience a little of something for a short time
4. tight contest	_____ to have a job to do
5. to run through	_____ to be able to enter or go into
6. to fight to the death	_____ to assemble something, to put something together
7. bush life	_____ a very close competition
8. spend time with	_____ to go through a series of activities; to do a series of activities
9. to have access	_____ to fight until there is only one clear winner or only one survivor
10. to get a taste	_____ life in the wild, in an undeveloped part of a country
11. from across the world	_____ to pass the time with

SPEAKING 2

Communication Focus 6: Giving Complex Descriptions

We can use an adjective clause (also called a relative clause) to describe a noun or pronoun, and in this way provide a more complete description. **Examples:**

> A coach is a person <u>who advises, helps, and trains people</u>.
>
> If you find a job <u>which you enjoy</u>, you will never work a day in your life.

Grammar Note: Relative Pronouns

The relative pronouns *who*, *whom**, *that*, and *whose* can introduce relative clauses referring to people.

who, whom, or whose	that	No Relative Pronoun**
The woman **who** lives next door is a professor.	The woman **that** lives next door is a professor.	The woman I met is a professor.
The man **whom*** you talked to used to be an accountant.	The man **that** you talked to used to be an accountant.	The man you talked to used to be an accountant.
The man **whose** wife is the CEO of the company has retired.		

*The use of *whom* is rare in conversation, although it is grammatically correct.
**When the relative pronoun can be left out, leave it out. This is most common in speaking and writing.

Which and *that* can introduce relative clauses referring to things.

which	that	No Relative Pronoun
The occupations **which** will have the most openings in the next 10 years are in the computer and health-care fields.	The occupations **that** will have the most openings in the next 10 years are in the computer and health-care fields.	The occupation (which/that) I would like to work in requires a master's degree.

👥 SPEAKING ACTIVITY 12

Work with a partner. Give definitions of the following professions. Use relative clauses. When you have finished, think of five additional occupations. Join another group and tell them your occupations. Together choose the two most interesting or unusual occupations and definitions and report to the class.

Example:

interviewer

An interviewer is a person who interviews people on television or radio. An interviewer may also be someone who interviews people for jobs.

1. funster
2. gangster
3. counsellor
4. interpreter
5. author
6. software engineer

7. lawyer
8. winemaker
9. server
10. novelist
11. designer
12. pharmacist

SPEAKING ACTIVITY 13

Work in a group. Explain what the following objects are and what they do. Use relative clauses. If you aren't sure, guess. Try to come up with two more of your own. Then check your answers with another group.

Example:

A can opener is a tool which we use to open cans.

Item	Answer/Guess	Correct?
1. a folder		
2. a blender		
3. a bestseller		
4. a money-maker		
5. a lawn mower		
6. a tear-jerker		

Communication Focus 7:
Adding Information and Ideas to Maintain Conversation

These expressions add information and ideas, and may help to keep a conversation going.

Structures/Expressions

I'd like to add . . .   And besides that . . .

What's more . . .   And in addition . . .*

Furthermore . . .   And moreover . . .*

Yes, and to take that a little further . . .

*And in addition . . . and And moreover . . . are used mostly in writing; they are very formal sounding and rarely used in speaking.

SPEAKING ACTIVITY 14

Work with a partner and interview him or her about work. When you answer give additional information using the expressions above. Report to the class on the most interesting information you found out.

1. Do you have a job? What is it?
2. What is your dream job? Explain why you would like this job.
3. What's your idea of a terrible job?
4. Would you rather work for a male boss or a female boss? Explain why.
5. What do you think is the best way to find a job?
6. If you didn't have to work, would you work anyway? Why?
7. What kind of work do you think you will be doing 10 years from now?
8. What is more important—making a lot of money or really enjoying your job?
9. How many careers or occupations do you think you will have in your lifetime?
10. Do you think there is equal opportunity for everyone in the work place? Why?
11. What do you think about self-employment or freelancing as ways of earning a living?
12. Do you think men and women should get the same salaries for the same work?
13. If you could own your own business, what kind of business would you like to have?
14. Are there any jobs that you think women are better at than men? What jobs are men better at?
15. At what age would you like to retire? What would you like to do after retirement?

Communication Focus 8: Describing Skills, Knowledge, and Abilities

In addition to *can/could/be able to,* there are other ways of describing skills, knowledge, and abilities. We do this by using a question word + an infinitive.
Example:

I know how to swim.

Structures/Expressions	Examples
. . . know how to . . .	She knows how to drive a truck.
. . . understand when to . . .	They understand when to turn the machine on.
. . . study what to . . .	She studied what to do in an emergency.
. . . learn where to . . .	He learned where to find the biggest fish.
. . . discover how long to . . .	She discovered how long to run the program.

👤👤👤 SPEAKING ACTIVITY 15

Work in a group of four. Make a quick chart with the headings shown below. Find out about each other. Each person should tell the group about two things he or she knows how to do very well and two things he or she would like to learn how to do. Make suggestions about how to learn to do the activities mentioned by the group.

Name	Knows how to . . .	Wants to learn . . .	Suggestions

Communication Focus 9: Interrupting

In the give-and-take of normal conversation, people may interrupt each other. It's important to use structures or expressions to let others know that you want to interrupt.

Structures/Expressions

Excuse me, may (can) I interrupt?   Do you mind if I interrupt?

Pardon me, I'd like to say something.

Can I interrupt?*

Could I jump in?*

*These are less formal

👤👤👤 SPEAKING ACTIVITY 16

Work in a group of five. Four of you will play the interrupting game and one person will be the scorekeeper who records the number of interruptions per person. Use two dice. Toss the dice to see who will speak first, second, etc. The first person to speak then tosses the dice. The number that comes up on the dice determines the topic. This person then gives an impromptu talk on that topic for two minutes. The other group members interrupt with valid questions. The person who successfully handles the most interruptions is the winner.

Number	Topic
2	Something I know how to do
3	The easiest job in the world
4	The most difficult job in the world
5	What I would like to learn how to do
6	My strengths—what I am good at

PRONUNCIATION

Pronunciation Focus: More on Linking

In normal fast speech in English, we often link the end of one word to the following word. This may cause a change in pronunciation. Pronunciation changes occur under four conditions.

 PRONUNCIATION ACTIVITY 1

 **Track 69**   **Condition 1:** When a word ending with / t / is followed by a word beginning with / y /, the resulting sound is pronounced / tʃ / as in the first and last sounds in **ch**ur**ch**.

A. Listen to the following phrases and write each one.

1. _____

2. _____

3. _____

4. _____

5. _____

6. _____

7. _____

8. _____

9. _____

10. _____

11. _____

12. _____

13. _____

B. Check your work with a partner. Practise repeating the sentences to each other.

PRONUNCIATION ACTIVITY 2

Condition 2: When a word ending in / d / is followed by a word beginning with / y /, the resulting sound is pronounced as / dʒ / as in the first and last sounds in ju**dg**e.

 **Track 70**

A. Listen to each sentence, and then write it.

1. _____
2. _____
3. _____
4. _____
5. _____
6. _____
7. _____
8. _____
9. _____
10. _____
11. _____
12. _____
13. _____
14. _____

B. Check your work with a partner, and then repeat the sentences to each other.

PRONUNCIATION ACTIVITY 3

Work with a partner. Make up a question using phrases with / tʃ / or / dʒ / for each of the answers. Then practise saying the question and answers.

1. _____?

   I bought this dress at a flea market.

2. _____?

   I came here last year.

3. _____?

   I put your hat on the shelf.

4. _____?

   I met that young woman in an English class.

5. _____?

   No, but I ate breakfast this morning.

6. _____?

As a matter of fact, I didn't like the play at all.

7. _____?

Sure. I'd be happy to sit down.

8. _____?

I took a cab.

9. _____?

I went to the library and I went alone.

10. _____?

I called you at seven o'clock because I wanted your help.

👥 PRONUNCIATION ACTIVITY 4

Work with a partner. Make up a dialogue using as many phrases with / tʃ / or / dʒ / as you can. Your dialogue should be logical and natural sounding.

👤 PRONUNCIATION ACTIVITY 5A

🎧 Track 71

Condition 3: When a tense vowel (/ iy /, / ey /, / uw /, / ow /, / ɑ /, / ɔy /, / ɑy /, / ɑw /) is followed by a word that begins with a vowel, the words are linked by the semi-vowel sounds / y / or / w /.

Listen to each phrase. Write the phrase, and then write the sound you hear linking the words.

1. Do it. **(w)** _____
2. See Ann. **(y)** _____
3. _____
4. _____
5. _____
6. _____
7. _____
8. _____
9. _____
10. _____
11. _____
12. _____

👤 PRONUNCIATION ACTIVITY 5B

 Track 72

Listen a second time and repeat the phrases.

PRONUNCIATION ACTIVITY 6

Condition 4: When a tense vowel (/ iy /, / ey /, / uw /, / ow /, / ɑ /, / ɔy /, / ɑy /, / ɑw /) is followed by a word which begins with a semi-vowel (/ w /, / y /), the semi-vowel is pronounced as one long sound.

 **Track 73**

A. Listen to these phrases and repeat.

1. be young
2. free university
3. say yes
4. go where
5. do one
6. see yesterday
7. blue water
8. try yellow

B. Practise saying the phrases with a partner.

PRONUNCIATION ACTIVITY 7

Work with a partner. Make up three dialogues using the kinds of linking as described in the four conditions listed above. Role-play your dialogues for the class.

PRONUNCIATION ACTIVITY 8

A. It's important for English learners to understand linking and reductions, but it's not necessary to try to speak that way in the beginning. Listen and write out the sentences that you hear.

Track 74

1. _____
2. _____
3. _____
4. _____
5. _____
6. _____
7. _____
8. _____
9. _____
10. _____
11. _____
12. _____
13. _____
14. _____
15. _____

B. Check your sentences with a partner. Then practise saying them to each other.

COMMUNICATING IN THE REAL WORLD

Use your English to talk to people outside your classroom. On your own or with a partner, talk to five people outside your class. Make up your own questions based on the topics in this chapter or ask the questions below and record the information.

Make a short report to the class about what you learned.

Here is one way to introduce your assignment.

> Could I ask you some questions? I am doing an assignment for my English class.

1. In your day-to-day activities, is it your head (your mind) or your heart (your emotions and feelings) that guides you to make decisions?
2. What's your job? How do you feel about it?
3. What do you think is the most difficult job in the world? What is the easiest?
4. What is your dream job?
5. What skills would you like to learn how to do?
6. What are you most afraid of?
7. What are you most worried about?

SELF-EVALUATION

Think about your work in this chapter. For each row in the chart sections **Grammar and Language Functions**, **Learning Strategies**, and **Pronunciation**, give yourself a score based on the rating scale below and write a comment in the Notes section.

Show the chart to your teacher. Talk about what you need to do to make your English better.

Rating Scale

1	2	3	4	5

Needs improvement. ←———————————————→ *Great!*

	Score	Notes
Grammar and Language Functions		
expressing assumptions and probability in the present and the past		
expressing emotions		
making and responding to suggestions		
apologizing and responding to apologies		
giving complex descriptions using relative pronouns		
adding information and ideas to maintain conversation		
describing skills, knowledge, and abilities		
interrupting		
Pronunciation		
comprehending and pronouncing linked sounds in English phrases		
Learning Strategies		
Speaking		
using attending behaviours to let the listener know I am supportive and paying attention, to encourage conversation		
acknowledging questions and letting the listener know that I am getting ready to answer the question		
Listening		
identifying key words to help me understand what the listening is about		
evaluating my ability to follow the main ideas and details to help me better manage my problem areas in listening		

Vocabulary and Language Chunks
Look at this list of new vocabulary and language chunks you learned in this chapter. Give yourself a score based on the rating scale and write a comment.

to be delighted	to put something together	to fight to the death
to turn someone on	to have drive	bush life
to turn someone off	to hold a competition	spend time with
to get in the way	to face a task	to have access
to get something done	to pull something together	to get a taste
to get better at	tight contest	from across the world
to turn out	to run through	to tune in

	Score	Notes
understanding new vocabulary and language chunks		
using new words and phrases correctly		

Write eight sentences and use new vocabulary you learned in this chapter.

1. _____
2. _____
3. _____
4. _____
5. _____
6. _____
7. _____
8. _____

My plan for practising is _____

_____

_____

_____

CHAPTER 7

Understanding Differences

Society and Culture

Making recommendations and predicting consequences

Restating and hesitating

Making complaints

Expressing warnings and prohibitions

THINKING AND TALKING

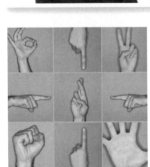

Do this quiz about gestures around the world. Compare your answers with a partner. Your teacher will give you the correct answers.

1. The okay gesture is considered _____.
    a. rude in Brazil
    b. rude in England
    c. rude in Canada and the US

2. Pulling down the far corner of your eye with the index or middle finger in France means _____.
    a. I like looking at you
    b. I am going to cry
    c. I do not believe you

3. Curling your index finger towards you to summon someone is _____.
    a. very insulting in some Asian countries
    b. a compliment in Singapore
    c. not polite in North America

4. Standing with hands on the hips is an expression of _____.
    a. openness and self-confidence in North America
    b. hostility in Mexico
    c. both of the above

5. The thumbs-up gesture signals _____.
    a. all is well/very good in Iran
    b. all is well/very good in North America
    c. a polite gesture in some Middle Eastern countries

6. If you sit with the soles of your feet or shoes showing you will insult _____.
    a. people from some Middle Eastern countries
    b. people from Thailand
    c. both of the above

7. Tipping the head backward and making a clicking sound with the tongue means _____.
    a. "no" to people from Saudi Arabia and other Middle Eastern countries
    b. "Let's have a drink" to people from Finland
    c. "Good job" to people from Europe

8. Holding the outstretched hand up in front of someone means _____.
    a. "May I speak?" in some Asian countries
    b. "May I have this dance?" in Argentina
    c. "I don't like you" in Germany

LISTENING 1: THE DO'S AND TABOOS OF BODY LANGUAGE—AN INTERVIEW

Before You Listen

👤👤👤 Pre-listening Activity

Work in a group of three. What gestures do people use here and in other countries to send the following messages?

Meaning	Gesture	
	Here	Other Countries
to show agreement		
to show uncertainty		
to get the server's attention in a restaurant		
to beckon to someone		
to point something out		
to get someone to speak louder		
to find out if someone is speaking to you		
to greet someone		
to get someone's attention		

👤👤 Pre-listening Vocabulary

A. You will hear an interview on the audio CD that includes the following vocabulary. Work with a partner or by yourself to write the correct word next to its definition in the chart on the next page.

taboo	intimidating	limp	to bribe	veteran
nuances	to flash	subtle	to beckon	derogatory
harmless	innocent	globetrotter	bumbling	universal
to waggle	to whistle	to boo	symbol	

Definitions	Vocabulary
1. world traveller	globetrotter
2. weak; lacking force; not stiff or firm	
3. to give money to persuade someone to do something illegal	
4. to send a quick signal	
5. frightening; threatening	
6. slight; delicate; faint; indirect	
7. to call someone by a gesture	
8. something forbidden; a prohibition	
9. disrespectful, showing a low opinion of	
10. not intended to hurt or harm	
11. without danger or risk	
12. experienced person; old hand	
13. very slight differences; very subtle differences	
14. something that stands for or represents another thing	
15. to move with short quick movements from side to side or up and down	
16. in a confused way; showing no skill	
17. worldwide; known all over the world	
18. to make a clear high sound by forcing air through a small opening in the lips	
19. to make a sound which expresses strong disapproval	

B. Choose the correct words from the list above to fill in the blanks in these sentences. Use each word only once. Not all the words are used in the sentences. Please make changes to verbs or nouns when necessary.

1. Roger Axtel has travelled all over the world. He's a real _____globetrotter_____.

2. Could you please _____ to the waiter? I've been trying to get him to come over here but he isn't paying attention to me.

3. In some countries whistling at a performer is very _____.

4. In North America talking about religion or politics is not usually done. It's _____.

5. He tried _____ the manager to get him a better table. He _____ a twenty-dollar bill at him.

6. She's been reporting about foreign affairs for over 20 years. She's a _____ reporter.

7. Everyone thinks he's confused and disorganized, and often makes mistakes. They say he's a _____ old fool.

8. It can be difficult to understand the little differences or _____ of greetings in other cultures.

9. There's nothing wrong with smiling. It's an _____ and _____ gesture.

10. When Anna fainted her body became _____ and she fell to the floor.

11. The students were afraid of the police officer. He was very _____.

12. Don't worry. That big dog won't hurt you. He's quite _____.

Listening for the Main Ideas

Listen to the interview once and answer the questions.   🎧 **Track 75**

1. What are the main topics in the interview? Put a check mark next to each of the main points that the speakers discuss.
   a. books about cultural differences
   b. gestures used in Japan
   c. differences in handshakes
   d. gestures that fathers teach children
   e. gestures to get attention in a restaurant
   f. gestures using the fingers and hand
   g. gestures that might be rude in some countries but not in others
   h. universal gestures

2. What is the main idea of this interview?

Listening STRATEGY 👂
Try to guess the meaning of phrases you do not understand by using your knowledge of the context and your background knowledge.

Listening Comprehension

A. Read the headings below. They are the most important ideas discussed during the interview.   🎧 **Track 76**

B. Listen to the interview again. As you listen, take notes about all the details that you hear under each heading. You can listen as many times as necessary to add more details to your notes.

What to do if you don't understand the language

_____

_____

_____

Roger Axtel

_____

_____

_____

Differences in handshakes

_____

_____

_____

Getting service in a restaurant

_____

_____

_____

Differences in the meaning of whistling

_____

_____

The okay gesture

_____

_____

_____

Universally understood gesture

_____

_____

_____

C. Check your notes with a partner and your teacher.

Personalizing

A. Work in a group of three or four. Talk about the following topics. Make sure that everyone contributes to the discussion. Choose someone to report to the class.

1. What new information did you learn from listening to the interview with Roger Axtel?

2. What are some surprising North American gestures or customs?

3. How important is body language, in your opinion?

B. Work with a partner and discuss these questions. Report to the class.

1. What is culture? What are some things that define a culture?

2. What are the most important values in your culture (for example, family)?

3. What is considered rude in your culture? What is considered polite in your culture?

4. How are young people in your culture different from young people here? Why is that?

5. In English there is a saying "When in Rome, do as the Romans do." What do you think it means? Do you think this is good advice?

Speaking STRATEGY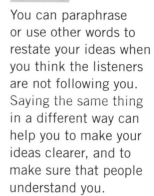

You can paraphrase or use other words to restate your ideas when you think the listeners are not following you. Saying the same thing in a different way can help you to make your ideas clearer, and to make sure that people understand you.

VOCABULARY AND LANGUAGE CHUNKS

Write the number of each expression next to its meaning. After checking your answers, choose six expressions and write your own sentences.

Expressions

1. handy-dandy
2. not to work
3. to keep it simple
4. off the top of my head
5. to get someone into trouble
6. to look someone in the eye
7. to catch on
8. back and forth
9. to fall back on
10. to go abroad
11. to stick with
12. to get back to
13. to make sense

Meanings

_____ to resort to; to be able to use in an emergency

_____ to understand, get the message

_____ without thinking too much about something

_____ backward and forward, to and fro

_____ to travel to other countries

_____ to put someone into a situation for which they will be criticized, blamed, or punished

_____ to make direct eye contact with someone

_____ to make the message clear, plain, and uncomplicated

_____ not to succeed

___1___ convenient, useful, and very good

_____ to be understandable, justifiable, reasonable

_____ to stay with; to continue with

_____ to return to

SPEAKING 1

Communication Focus 1: Making Recommendations and Predicting Consequences

You give a recommendation when you tell someone that you think a certain action should or should not happen. The consequences are what happens as a result of the action. Here are some structures we can use to make recommendations and to predict the consequences of not following the recommendations.

Structures/Expressions	Examples
If . . . , will . . .	If you show the soles of your feet in Thailand, you will insult people. If you use inappropriate body language, people will think you are rude.
It's a good idea to . . . or . . .	It's a good idea to maintain eye contact in conversation or the other person will think you are not interested in the conversation.
It's not a good idea to . . . or else . . .	It's not a good idea to burp loudly when you finish your meal or else people will think you are rude.
. . . should . . . or . . .	You should stand about three feet away from people or they will feel uncomfortable.
. . . should not . . . or (else . . .)	You shouldn't dress too formally for the party or else you'll look out of place.
I recommend/suggest that . . .*	I recommend that she apologize or else they will be very angry.

*This is the most formal usage.

Please note that we use the subjunctive form of the verb after *recommend* or *suggest*. The subjunctive looks like the base form of the verb and is used with all subjects. The exception is the verb *to be*. The subjunctive of *to be* is *were*. We can use it with all subjects.

Grammar Note: Conditional Sentences Referring to Future Time

Sentences with *if* clauses are conditional sentences. In conditional sentences referring to future time, we use the present tense in the *if* clause. The order of the clauses can be reversed with no change in meaning.
Examples:

> If you wave at the waiter, you will get his attention.
>
> You will get the waiter's attention if you wave at him.

👥 SPEAKING ACTIVITY 1

Work with a partner. Make two recommendations and predict consequences in these situations. An example for each situation has been provided.

Eating a meal in a restaurant
Example:

1. **You shouldn't drink your soup from your soup bowl or else people will think you are rude.**

2. _____

3. _____

In a classroom
Example:

1. It's not a good idea to look at another student's work or else the teacher will think you are cheating.

2. _____

3. _____

On a bus
Example:

1. If you stare at someone, you will make him or her feel very uncomfortable.

2. _____

3. _____

Other situation: _____

1. _____

2. _____

👥 SPEAKING ACTIVITY 2

Work in a group of three. What will people think if you do the following in other countries? Name the country and describe the consequences of the actions. Use complete sentences.

1. if you look a teacher or parent directly in the eye
2. if you point at someone or something
3. if you make the okay gesture
4. if you put your feet on a desk or table
5. if you beckon with your index finger
6. if you sit on the floor at a party or gathering
7. if you eat with your hands
8. if you come to a dinner party two hours late

Communication Focus 2: Restating and Hesitating

We use expressions to restate what someone has said to check our understanding or to gain time to think of an answer.

Structures/Expressions for Restating

So, what you are (he is/they are) saying is . . .

In other words . . .

If I understand you . . .

Do you mean . . .

Structures/Expressions for Hesitating

We can use expressions of hesitating to gain time to think of an answer to a question.

> **Well . . . Ah . . . Ummm . . . okay . . .**
>
> **That's a good point . . . /That's a good question . . .**
>
> **Let me see.**

Note: We can use these two language functions (hesitating and restating) together.

Example:

> **Well, let me see. So what you are saying is . . . that this job requires special training.**

🗣 SPEAKING ACTIVITY 3

Speaking STRATEGY 💬

Try to add information and ideas during a conversation. This will help to keep the conversation going. Here are two expressions to use:

> I'd like to add . . .
> Can I add something?

Customs regarding dating and marriage differ from culture to culture. Work with a partner. Take turns interviewing each other. Use hesitating and restating expressions in your answers. Report to the class.

1. What is an important cultural difference between your hometown and this city?
2. Are there any differences between men and women in North America and men and women in your home country?
3. How do people meet and arrange dates in your home country? Who does the inviting? Do people go on blind dates?
4. Who should pay when a couple is out on a date? Explain why.
5. What happens at a wedding ceremony in your home country? How do people celebrate?
6. Why do people look forward to getting married?
7. Do people have to fall in love before they get married?
8. Is it better to be single or to be married?
9. Describe your ideal partner.

Communication Focus 3: Making Complaints

In North American English, speakers can make direct or indirect complaints. The purpose of a direct complaint is to bring about a change. Direct complaints can have four parts.

Complaint Formulas	Examples
1. Explanation of reason for complaint	I just wanted to see you to talk about my exam.
2. Complaint	In my opinion, my mark was a bit too low.
3. Justification, explanation	I really studied a lot for the exam and I knew all the answers. Maybe I didn't always use the right words in my answers.
4. Request (for solution or repair)	I would really appreciate it if you could go over my paper and reconsider the marks you gave me.

If you expect a positive outcome, your complaint should include the following elements:

Elements of a Complaint	Examples
depersonalization of the problem	My mark was a bit too low. (**not** "You gave me a very low mark.")
a request with a modal such as *could* or *would*	Could you re-mark my paper? (**not** "You didn't mark my paper accurately.")
avoidance of blame and criticism	I wanted to talk about my exam. (not "The mark you gave me was too low.")

🗣 SPEAKING ACTIVITY 4

Work with a partner. Organize the sentences in each dialogue so that they are in the correct order. Then, choose one dialogue and practise saying it.

Dialogue 1

_____ Miguel: Could you please, because I can't put up with this phone much longer.

_____ Miguel: No, not really. Actually, could I just exchange it for a less complicated model?

_____ Miguel: Well, it is very complicated and lights keep flashing all the time, and I really don't think it's straightforward enough for me to use. I keep getting my voicemail and text messages late, and I don't know how to adjust it to keep it working properly.

_____ Miguel: Hi, I wanted to talk to you about a cellphone I bought here last week.

_____ Salesperson: I'm not sure I can do that. It depends on your contract, but I can check that for you.

_____ Salesperson: Sure. Anything wrong with it?

_____ Salesperson: I see. Do you want me to go over it with you?

Dialogue 2

_____ Supervisor: I'm not sure I can. All the offices are occupied.

_____ Supervisor: Okay, let me see what I can do. Maybe I can find an empty office on another floor.

_____ Supervisor: I see. Have you thought of keeping the door open?

_____ Supervisor: Sure. Is there anything I can do about it?

_____ Maria: It doesn't seem to make any difference. Could you move me to an office that has better ventilation?

_____ Maria: But . . . it's very important that my clients and I have a space which doesn't give us headaches.

_____ Maria: I hope so, because the air is so stale that both the clients and I get terrible headaches after less than an hour in that room.

_____ Maria: I'm sorry to bother you, but I want to speak to you about the air in my office.

👥 SPEAKING ACTIVITY 5

Work with a partner. In which of the following situations would you make a complaint? What result would you hope for? Choose two complaints and role-play them. Use the complaint formula.

Situation	Would you complain or not?	What is the result you would hope for?
1. You got a very low mark on an essay that took a long time to research and write.		
2. You bought a pair of waterproof winter boots, but when you wore them you found that they leaked.		
3. The pizza you ordered was delivered late and with completely different toppings than the ones you asked for.		
4. One of the students in your class was very rude to you and called you a rude name.		
5. The neighbours above you have loud parties most Saturday nights.		
6. A lot of people at school wear perfume or cologne, and you are allergic to it.		
7. You went to a movie during which the audience made so much noise that you missed half of the dialogue.		
8. You received a lower mark in a speaking test than you expected, but everyone says your speaking is excellent.		

👥 SPEAKING ACTIVITY 6

Work in a group of three. Make a quick chart with the headings shown on the next page. Talk about the last time you made a complaint. Compare your complaints with those of another group and report the most interesting complaints to the class.

	What did you complain about?	Who did you complain to?	What did you say?	What was the result?
Name				

Communication Focus 4: Expressing Warnings and Prohibitions

We use *had better* to express strong advice or warning. *Or else* is used to predict the consequences likely to occur if the warning is not listened to.

We use *mustn't* to express prohibition. This means that something is not permitted by law or is against the rules.

Structures/Expressions	Examples
. . . had better . . . . . . or else . . .	You **had better go** to the interview on time **or else** you won't get the job.
	You **had better not stare** at people **or else** they will think you are rude.
. . . mustn't . . .	You **mustn't lie** on your resumé.
	You **mustn't borrow** something without the owner's permission.

Other Structures to Express Prohibition

It's illegal to . . . **It's illegal** to make and sell alcohol.

It's against the law to . . . **It's against the law** to copy and sell books and movies.

. . . isn't allowed . . . Copying and selling music **isn't allowed** in North America.

Speaking STRATEGY

If you ask questions during a conversation, this will help to keep the conversation going.
Examples:
Excuse me, I have a question . . .
By the way, . . .
Can you explain . . .
What do you mean . . .

👥 SPEAKING ACTIVITY 7

Work in a group of three. Imagine you are writing a guide book for tourists to three countries you know very well. Tell people three things they **mustn't do** and three things they **had better** or **had better not do** in those countries. Predict the consequences of those actions. Report your ideas to the class.

Country	Prohibitions	Warnings	Consequences
Canada	You mustn't drive without a licence.	You had better not park in a bicycle lane,	or else you will get a ticket.

SPEAKING ACTIVITY 8

Work with a partner. Interview each other and report the most interesting information or opinions to the class. Ask questions to keep the conversation going.

1. Do you believe in capital punishment? Why or why not?
2. Do you think we need stricter laws or punishment?
3. Do you think people should be able to freely copy books, movies, and music? Why or why not?
4. How do you feel about the police? Are you afraid of them/do you dislike them? Why?
5. Do you think governments have the right to ban certain habits such as smoking or using drugs?
6. Do you think there is more crime now than 10 years ago?
7. Do you feel safe on the streets of your city?
8. Some people who have defended themselves during break-ins or robberies have been charged by the police. What do you think of this?
9. Do parents have the right to physically discipline their children? Why or why not?
10. Are there any crimes which you think should not be illegal? Please explain.

LISTENING 2: COPYRIGHT LAWS— A DOCUMENTARY REPORT

Before You Listen

🚶 Pre-listening Activity 1

Discuss these questions with your partner.

1. What are some laws which exist in some countries but not in others?
2. Have you ever broken the law? Please explain.
3. It is against the law to copy books, music, or movies without paying for them. What is your opinion on this issue?

🚶 Pre-listening Activity 2

Read this overview of the listening with a partner. Discuss the questions below.

Copyright is the legal right of the person who creates a work to keep it as his property or to distribute or sell his creation. Some people agree with this and believe that the creation is the "intellectual property" of the artist who created it. No one can copy it or distribute it without permission.

Other people think that the creations of artists belong to all of society and that everyone should be able to use them, because today we have more tools than ever before to create and communicate ideas.

The first copyright law was passed by the English Parliament. The purposes of the law were to pay artists for their works and to encourage them to create more.

The writers of the American constitution followed the same ideas as the English, but they didn't like giving anyone the right to control knowledge and ideas, so the American government gave out copyrights which lasted only for a limited time.

Copyright laws today have expanded greatly. Today, copyright is similar to complete ownership. Large corporations control copyright and make a lot of money from it. They want even stronger copyright laws.

Society needs intellectual property rights to protect creators but it also needs to allow people to build up the knowledge networks on which the future depends. There needs to be a balance between how much copyright laws control and the creation, development, and spread of new knowledge networks.

1. What is copyright?
2. Does everyone agree about copyright laws? Why or why not?

3. How did copyright laws start in North America?
4. How have copyright laws changed since the early days?
5. What problems has the change caused?

👥 Pre-listening Vocabulary

A. You will hear an interview on the audio CD that includes the following vocabulary. Work with a partner or by yourself to write the correct word next to its definition in the chart below.

theft	patronage	absurd	principles
digital	patent	acute	statute
massive	controversial	shift	mishmash
morality	temporary	significance	monopoly
extensive	incidence	vast	livelihood
licence	public domain	sanity	stringent
potential	to determine	royalties	knowledge economy

Definitions	Vocabulary
1. law	statute
2. importance; meaningfulness	
3. something which the public can use; something which is part of the culture and not protected by copyright	
4. a system of values and rules of conduct	
5. collection of unrelated things; mixed up together	
6. the ownership or control of something by one person or one company	
7. financial support provided to artists and writers by patrons or supporters	
8. causing arguments; causing people to debate about a topic	
9. document giving official permission to do something	
10. the right given by government to use or sell a creation	
11. to decide; to settle; to shape or to influence	
12. strict, severe; following the rules exactly	
13. an economy based on creating and trading knowledge and ideas	
14. money paid by a publisher to the writer or creator of a work	
15. large in amount or extending over a large area	
16. only for a limited time period; not permanent	
17. a move	

18. ridiculous; crazy; illogical	
19. occurrence or number of times something happens	
20. very great in size	
21. possible; capable of becoming fact	
22. sharp; strong; severe	
23. a way of making a living; source of income	
24. rules, beliefs, or values that help you know right from wrong	
25. describing the process of storing data, images, sounds, etc., by using groups of electronic bits	
26. a sound, healthy mind	
27. huge; enormous; gigantic	
28. robbery; stealing	

B. Choose the correct words from the list above to fill in the blanks in these sentences. Use each word only once. Not all the words are used in the sentences. Please make changes to verbs or nouns when necessary.

1. Some people have been copying a great many books and lots of music. They have been doing this on a ____massive____ scale.

2. Today there is a very high _____ of people breaking copyright.

3. Eric Flint is a writer whose living or _____ depends on _____ or the money he makes from sales of his books.

4. The Internet has provided the possibility or _____ for people to make extremely large or _____ amounts of money.

5. The first American copyright law only protected works for a short time. It was _____.

6. Before this law, writers made a living through the _____ or the support of the aristocracy.

7. The first copyright laws tried to encourage writers and artists to add to the _____ _____ of ideas.

8. We are in a new kind of economy in which the ability to make ideas and knowledge is more important than the ability to manufacture steel or plastics. It's called a _____ _____.

9. Copyright laws are very _____. People disagree about them.

10. Writers and their publishers call their works intellectual property, but some people think this is _____. It doesn't make sense because ideas are not really property.

11. There has been a sharp or _____ increase in illegal copying recently.

Listening for the Main Ideas

 **Track 77**

Listen to the report once and answer the questions.

1. What are the main points of view about copyright that are discussed in the program?
2. Why has the issue of copyright laws become so important?
3. Who owns ideas, according to the narrator? Why?

Listening Comprehension

Track 78

A. Read the nine questions below.
B. Listen to the report again. As you listen, take notes about all the details that you hear that will help you answer the questions later.

Listening STRATEGY

Mentally summarizing the main points a speaker makes will help you to understand the listening better.

1. What is the copy fight? What are the opposing sides?
2. How does the entertainment industry feel about copyright laws? Why?
3. Why are growing numbers of people against copyright laws?
4. The narrator says we are at a crisis or turning point. Why is this?
5. What was the purpose of copyright laws in the beginning?
6. Why did the US constitution permit lawmakers to pass copyright laws?
7. How has copyright changed today?
8. What does an information society need?
9. What is the narrator's opinion of the copyright issue?

Track 79

C. Listen as many times as necessary to add more details to your notes in Part B. Check your notes with a partner.

Personalizing

Listening STRATEGY

Taking notes focuses your attention and helps you follow the key ideas in a listening text.

A. Work in a small group. Discuss these questions and try to reach consensus. Make a list of reasons to support your opinions.

1. Should society should make and enforce stronger copyright laws?
2. Should manufacturers be allowed to copy brand-name clothing, handbags, jewellery, etc.?
3. Should writers be allowed to use other peoples' words, expressions, and story ideas?

B. Debate on Copyright Laws

The class can break up into two groups—those who support stronger copyright laws and are against copying, and those who think there should be free sharing of information, ideas, and intellectual property.

Each group will make a list of its arguments and reasons.

The groups will take turns presenting their arguments and responding to the other side's arguments. Each group's purpose is to persuade the other side that its opinion is correct and the other side is wrong.

A chairperson (student or teacher) oversees the whole activity and makes sure that the debate is respectful and balanced. One person acts as a timekeeper to make sure that each side sticks to the time given to it.

VOCABULARY AND LANGUAGE CHUNKS

Write the number of each expression next to its meaning. After checking your answers, choose six expressions and write your own sentences.

Expressions		Meanings
1.	to make the most of	_____	the point at which important changes or events occur
2.	wrong way to go	__1__	to make the best use of; to take advantage of
3.	a turning point	_____	in a definite way; in a direct manner
4.	a necessary evil	_____	the use or enjoyment of something without paying or working for it
5.	land grab	_____	not the correct method, way, or procedure
6.	at the root of	_____	something we do not like but have to accept
7.	the Internet age	_____	a fast acquisition of land or property by force
8.	a free ride	_____	the cause, source, or origin of
9.	flat out	_____	a time in which information travels around the world in seconds, on the World Wide Web; information age
10.	a major shift	_____	of a huge size, proportion; in a big way
11.	on a massive scale	_____	an important change
12.	to make a living	_____	to be able to understand something or to solve a problem
13.	to be convinced	_____	to earn enough money to pay for everything you need
14.	to figure out	_____	to be completely sure

PRONUNCIATION

Pronunciation Focus: Information Focus and Intonation

 **Track 80**   In conversations, the last content word in the sentence often receives the most emphasis. In this case, the rise or fall in intonation begins on the stressed syllable of this last content word. This is the word that the speaker thinks is the most important. This word is the information focus of the sentence.

Listen to the examples.

What are you <u>do</u>ing?   I'm taking a <u>break</u>.

You mustn't drive without a <u>licence</u>.   I got my licence <u>yes</u>terday.

Is it rude to use this <u>gesture</u>?   No, it's just <u>fine</u>.

Do you speak any other <u>languages</u>?   Yes, I speak <u>French</u>.

When the information focus is the last stressed content word in a sentence, this is called neutral focus, as in the sentences you just heard.

 PRONUNCIATION ACTIVITY 1

 **Track 81**   **A.** Listen to the sentences and underline the focus words.

1. Copyright is a controversial issue.
2. They want us to make the most of the new tools for communication.
3. File sharing is the illegal copying of music and movies.
4. The entertainment industry believes that they are the victims of theft.
5. Copyright determines who owns and controls the expression of ideas.
6. Staring at people is considered impolite.
7. Etiquette and manners differ from country to country.
8. Is it rude to use a cellphone in church?
9. Do corporations want to own intellectual property?
10. Does Eric Flint's livelihood depend on royalties?
11. Do people buy and sell ideas to make money in an information society?
12. Will stronger copyright laws help build a knowledge economy?
13. Do you think that copyright laws are a necessary evil?

B. Check your answers with a partner and the teacher. Then repeat these sentences to your partner in order to practise neutral focus.

C. Do a knuckle rap with your partner (touch your partner's knuckles with your own) as you say the focus word.

PRONUNCIATION ACTIVITY 2

As a conversation develops after the opening sentence, sometimes the focus changes to highlight new information. This depends on meaning and the context. In English, any word can receive focal stress.

 Track 82

A. Listen to the two dialogues. Then work with a partner to write another two dialogues in which the focus of the information changes.

Dialogue 1—At school

Andrew: You look ex**haust**ed.

Bianca: I went to a **par**ty last night.

Andrew: What **kind** of party?

Bianca: A **birth**day party.

Dialogue 2—In a restaurant

Server: What'll you **have**?

Customer: A **bagel**, a **toasted** bagel.

Server: Do you want any **cream** cheese?

Customer: No, **thanks**.

Server: Anything **else**?

Customer: **Coffee**, please.

B. Perform your dialogues for the class.

PRONUNCIATION ACTIVITY 3

Listen to the sentences, and circle the focus word. Check your answers.

Track 83

1. What's the matter with you?
2. How about Friday morning?
3. It's more important than verbal language.
4. Do you believe in it?
5. Did he look the principal in the eye?
6. I don't feel safe anywhere.
7. Do you want me to look at the ceiling when people are speaking?
8. Men don't hold hands with each other.
9. How far should he stand?
10. Is there anything else to stare at?

PRONUNCIATION ACTIVITY 4

Work with a partner. Circle what you think the focus word should be in the following sentences. Then decide which of the sentences in the previous exercise would make a good response to each sentence. Check your answers. Then practise these dialogues with your partner.

1. Andre: Could we possibly meet tomorrow morning?

   Beth: _____

2. Carlos: Most people are against capital punishment, but I don't know what to think.

   Rosa: _____

3. Laura: Is it alright for men to hold hands?

   Nelson: _____

4. Georgios: What's the matter?

   Anna: _____

5. Andrea: Don't stare at people in elevators.

   Brian: _____

6. Ellen: John stands too close to people.

   Lucy: _____

7. Abbas: It's not polite to look at the floor when someone is speaking.

   Summer: _____

8. Armando: He couldn't look the teacher in the eye.

   Edward: _____

9. Jonah: How important is non-verbal language?

   Diego: _____

10. Eli: Do you feel safe in the city?

    Elizabeth: _____

PRONUNCIATION ACTIVITY 5

Track 84

A. Listen to the conversational exchanges and underline the focus word in each sentence. How does change in focal stress in the sentence change the meaning?

   1. Andrew: Copyright is a controversial issue.

      Libby: True, but is it the most controversial issue?

   2. Serena: They want us to make the most of the new tools for communication.

      Jeff: Do they expect everyone to do that?

   3. Alex: File sharing is the illegal copying of music and movies.

      Lisa: What do you call the legal copying of music and movies?

   4. Judith: The entertainment industry believes that they are the victims of theft.

      Rosalie: But they don't know that they are the victims of theft.

   5. Rashida: Copyright determines who owns and controls the expression of ideas.

      Henry: I don't know how anyone can own ideas.

B. Check your answers and then practise the exchanges with a partner.

👥 PRONUNCIATION ACTIVITY 6

We use focus when we want to make contrasts. Listen to the examples in Part 1, and then, with a partner, underline the most prominent words in the contrasts in Part 2.  **Track 85**

Part 1

1. I found some **useful** information and some **useless** information.
2. He'd like a glass of **red** wine and I'll have **white** wine.
3. My cousin lives in London, **Ontario**, not London, **England**.
4. He has a terrible **headache**, not a **stomach ache**.
5. He told me he had some **good** news and some **bad** news.

Part 2

1. We live on the twelfth floor, not the twentieth floor.
2. They spent hundreds of dollars, not thousands.
3. He believes in freeing the expression of ideas, not controlling it.
4. People are free to both express and experience creativity.
5. The public, and not the creators, should own ideas in an information society.
6. Both teachers and students need to be responsible.
7. It's against the law to steal and to cheat.
8. Robin went to London, Ontario, but I went to London, England.
9. Under the law in Canada, men and women are treated equally.
10. Both her brother and her sister are famous actors.
11. Both Canada and the US are democracies.
12. Both Toronto and New York have stock markets.

👥 PRONUNCIATION ACTIVITY 7

A. Listen to the 12 contrast sentences in Part 2 of Pronunciation Activity 6 to check your answers.  **Track 86**

B. Practise saying the sentences with a partner and do a knuckle rap on the most prominent syllable of the contrasting words.
Example:

I live in an a<u>part</u>ment not in a <u>town</u>house.

👥 PRONUNCIATION ACTIVITY 8

A. We use focus when we want to contradict or correct a statement. Listen to the following examples.  **Track 87**

1. Her birthday is on January thirtieth.

   Really? I thought it was on January thirteenth.

2. Toronto is the capital of Canada.

   Are you sure? I think Ottawa is the capital.

3. The okay gesture is rude in the US.

   I don't think so. I think it's fine in the US.

4. Staring at people is polite in Canada and the US.

   Come on! It's rude to stare in Canada and the US.

B. Below you will see 11 sentences. Some are incorrect statements. Work with a partner to correct them. Here are some other expressions to use in your corrections:

Really?

I think that . . .

Are you sure?

I thought that . . .

I find that hard to believe.

Come on!

Example:

Marta: Shanghai is the capital of China.

Bjorn: Are you sure? I think that Beijing is the capital of China.

1. *Romeo and Juliet* was written by Hemingway.
2. Maintaining eye contact during conversation isn't important in the US and Canada.
3. San Francisco is the biggest city in the US.
4. All writers and artists want strong copyright laws.
5. People shake hands in the same way all over the world.
6. It's legal to spank children in every country.
7. The OK gesture is polite in all countries.
8. In Canada, it's legal to copy movies and sell them to your friends.
9. The US is as big as Canada.
10. People in Canada have a lot more money than people in the US.
11. The Americans passed the first copyright laws.

C. Practise saying the statements together using information focus stress to make the corrections.

COMMUNICATING IN THE REAL WORLD

Use your English to talk to people outside your classroom. On your own or with a partner, talk to five people outside your class. Make up your own questions based on the topics in this chapter or ask the questions below and record the information.

Make a short report to the class about what you learned.

Here is one way to introduce your assignment.

> Could I ask you some questions? I am doing an assignment for my English class.

1. What gestures or body language do you sometimes use?
2. What is a rude gesture in Canada?
3. What are some important values in this culture?
4. What do you like or dislike about this culture?
5. How do you feel about complaining? When was the last time you complained? What happened?

SELF-EVALUATION

Think about your work in this chapter. For each row in the chart sections **Grammar and Language Functions**, **Learning Strategies**, and **Pronunciation**, give yourself a score based on the rating scale below and write a comment in the Notes section.

Show the chart to your teacher. Talk about what you need to do to make your English better.

Rating Scale

1	2	3	4	5

Needs improvement. ←————————————————————→ *Great!*

	Score	Notes
Grammar and Language Functions		
making recommendations and predicting consequences		
restating and hesitating		
making complaints		
expressing warnings and prohibitions		
Pronunciation		
using information focus and intonation to send the right message		
Learning Strategies		
Speaking		
paraphrasing or restating to make sure that others understand		
adding information and ideas during a conversation, to help keep the conversation going		
asking questions during a conversation to keep the conversation going		
Listening		
trying to guess the meaning of phrases I do not understand by using the context and my background knowledge		
mentally summarizing the main points a speaker makes to help me to understand the listening		
taking notes to focus my attention and help me follow the key ideas in a listening text		

Vocabulary and Language Chunks

Look at this list of new vocabulary and language chunks you learned in this chapter. Give yourself a score based on the rating scale and write a comment.

handy-dandy	to stick with	a free ride
not to work	to get back to	flat out
to keep it simple	to make sense	a major shift
off the top of my head	to make the most of	to clog up
to get someone into trouble	wrong way to go	the Internet age
to look someone in the eye	a turning point	on a massive scale
to catch on	a necessary evil	to make a living
back and forth	land grab	to be convinced
to go abroad	at the root of	to figure out
to fall back on		

	Score	Notes
understanding new vocabulary and language chunks		
using new words and phrases correctly		

Write eight sentences and use new vocabulary you learned in this chapter.

1. _____
2. _____
3. _____
4. _____
5. _____
6. _____
7. _____
8. _____

My plan for practising is _____

_____

_____

_____

CHAPTER 8

Respecting Our World
Nature and the Environment

- Using the passive voice to ask for and give impersonal information
- Expressing disapproval and criticizing
- Expressing opinions with various degrees of certainty
- Expressing regrets
- Hypothesizing

THINKING AND TALKING

Read the following quote. Do you agree? Explain why or why not. Then brainstorm some changes that humans have made to earth's natural environment.

> Our ancestors viewed the Earth as rich and bountiful, which it is. Many people in the past also saw nature as inexhaustibly sustainable, which we now know is the case only if we care for it. . . .
>
> [The] exploration of outer space takes place at the same time as the Earth's own oceans, seas, and fresh water areas grow increasingly polluted. . . .
>
> Many of the Earth's habitats, animals, plants, insects . . . may not be known at all by future generations. We have the capability, and the responsibility. We must act before it is too late.
>
> —His Holiness Tenzin Gyatso, the Fourteenth Dalai Lama of Tibet, spiritual leader of the Tibetan Buddhist faith

SPEAKING 1

Speaking STRATEGY

When you are speaking, take a chance and try to express your ideas if you have something that you want to say. Don't worry about sounding foolish or making mistakes. The most important thing is to get your idea across.

SPEAKING ACTIVITY 1

A. Answer the questions on this survey about environmental values. Then work in a group of four to compare your results and explain your reasons. Report to the class about the percentage of people in your group that agreed and strongly agreed.

Questions	Strongly Agree	Agree Somewhat	Disagree
1. I love to be outdoors.			
2. Most kids do not spend enough time outdoors.			

3. Most kids these days care more about video games and their cellphones than about wildlife and clean air.			
4. Having a yard is important to me.			
5. Every town should have wide open land with nature trails nearby.			
6. Poisons in the environment shorten our lives.			
7. We need laws to protect large animals from extinction.			
8. I worry about the effects of environmental pollution on my family's health.			
9. Our children's lives will be worse because of our generation's wasteful habits.			
10. Taking good care of nature is part of our duty to God.			

Adapted from The American Environmental Values Survey's Environmental Consensus Points
http://ecoamerica.org/wp-content/uploads/2013/02/AEVS_Report.pdf

B. The results of the survey will be provided by your teacher. Read the results and compare the percentages in your group to those of the Americans in the survey. What differences or similarities are there? Why?

Communication Focus 1: Using the Passive Voice to Ask for and Give Impersonal Information

When we give impersonal information, we often use the passive voice. This focuses attention on the object or the person that received the action, not the person who performed the action.

Examples:

Active voice: The WWF (World Wildlife Fund) <u>raises</u> money to protect animals.

Passive voice: Money to protect animals <u>is raised</u> by the WWF.

Active: WWF-Canada (World Wildlife Fund Canada) <u>protects</u> 96 million acres of Canadian wilderness.

Passive: 96 million acres of Canadian wilderness <u>are protected</u> by WWF-Canada.

Active: Senator Alan MacNaughton <u>founded</u> WWF-Canada in 1967.

Passive: WWF-Canada <u>was founded</u> in 1967 by Senator Alan MacNaughton.

Grammar Note: The Passive Voice

Only verbs which can take objects can be used in the passive voice. In a passive sentence, the object of the verb in the active sentence becomes the subject of the passive verb.

The passive verb is formed by using the verb *to be* in the tense of the active sentence and the *past participle of the main verb* in the active sentence.

In the passive voice, a prepositional phrase starting with *by* indicates the doer of the action. This phrase is optional.

Active Sentence	Passive Sentence	Passive Sentence with the *by* Phrase
People speak English in North America.	English is spoken in North America.	English is spoken by people in North America.
100 years ago people spoke English in North America.	English was spoken in North America 100 years ago.	English was spoken by people in North America 100 years ago.
People have spoken English in North America for a long time.	English has been spoken in North America for a long time.	English has been spoken by people in North America for a long time.
People are going to speak English in North America in the future.	English is going to be spoken in North America in the future.	English is going to be spoken by people in North America in the future.
People should speak English in North America.	English should be spoken in North America.	English should be spoken by people in North America.
People are speaking English in North America.	English is being spoken in North America.	English is being spoken by people in North America.

SPEAKING ACTIVITY 2

Here's a list of statements from a press release about WWF-Canada. Work with a partner and change all the verbs in the active sentences to the passive voice. Then, choose the four that you think are the most important facts. Present your list to the class.

Facts about WWF-Canada

1. WWF-Canada supports research to protect Canadian wildlife and habitats.
2. WWF-Canada is setting up a network of protected marine areas.
3. They have tackled conservation challenges facing Canada.
4. They have developed recovery plans for whales in the St. Lawrence River.
5. WWF-Canada supports groups who want to save the natural world.

Past Successes

1. WWF-Canada has saved thousands of acres of tropical rain forests in South America.

2. They protected over 10 million hectares of wilderness in the Mackenzie River delta from industrial development.

3. With the help of a corporate sponsor, they took the white pelican off the endangered list.

4. They moved shipping lanes in the Bay of Fundy away from whale feeding grounds.

LISTENING 1: ELEPHANTS IN ZOOS— A RADIO INTERVIEW

Before You Listen

👥 Pre-listening Activity

Work with a partner and decide if these statements are true or false. State your opinions even if you are not sure. Share your opinions with the rest of the class. (The teacher will tell you the answers later.)

1. The elephant is the largest land animal.

2. Elephants die at about age 40 in captivity and in their 70s in the wild.

3. Elephants live in groups of females such as mothers, aunts, grandmothers, juveniles, and infants.

4. An adult elephant needs to walk around 50 kilometres per day in order to stay healthy.

5. Most zoos can't care for elephants properly because they don't give them enough space.

6. Elephants need approximately 100 acres of wide open space.

7. Male elephants are rarely seen in zoos because they are bigger and more aggressive, and need larger enclosures than the females.

8. Animal rights advocates are calling on all zoos to close down elephant exhibits and send the elephants to sanctuaries.

👥 Pre-listening Vocabulary

A. You will hear an interview on the audio CD that includes the following vocabulary. Work with a partner or by yourself to write the correct word next to its definition in the chart below.

minuscule	protocols	misguided	to breed
illicit	captivity	fragmentation	sham
appropriate	corral	marginally	welfare
to ban	facility	habitat	ivory trade
calf	to boost	horrendous	to raise
infection	herd	premise	dire
tusk	to overstate	conservation	

Definitions	Vocabulary
1. extremely small	minuscule
2. a baby elephant, or baby cow	
3. to forbid; to prohibit	
4. to collect money	
5. set of rules and procedures	
6. a pen or enclosure for large animals such as horses	
7. a disease carried by germs that enter the body	
8. to increase; to push up from below	
9. a group of animals that live together, such as cows	
10. a basic idea; a proposition	
11. very bad; extreme; urgent	
12. a long pointed tooth which extends outside the mouth, as in elephants or walruses	
13. to exaggerate, to say that something is bigger and more important than it is	
14. in a state of not being free; confinement	
15. a building or structure designed and built for a specific purpose	
16. mistaken; erroneous	
17. slightly; a tiny bit	
18. broken into pieces or fragments; disintegration, destruction	
19. home; environment	
20. a deception; pretense; fraud	
21. to cause to reproduce	
22. health and well being	
23. illegal, unlawful; criminal	
24. awful; terrible; dreadful	
25. trade in the tusks of elephants	
26. correct; right	
27. protection and preservation; keeping safe from harm	

B. Choose the correct vocabulary from the list above to fill in the blanks in these sentences. Use each word only once. Not all the words are used in the sentences. Please make changes to verbs or nouns when necessary.

1. The baby elephant's chances of surviving are very small. They're _____minuscule_____.

2. After I cut myself the doctor gave me some medicine to prevent _____.

3. An elephant's _____ needs to be extensive because these animals have to have a lot of room.

4. It's difficult for some animals to reproduce in zoos. They don't often _____ in _____.

5. Even though the _____ is illegal, many gangs still hunt elephants and sell their _____ and bones on the black market.

6. Animal activists are worried about the lives and _____ of animals in zoos.

7. Groups of animals such as elephants live together in _____ and are often kept in a special _____ or pen in zoos.

8. The Calgary Zoo built a large modern _____ to house their elephants.

9. Animal activists say that the amount of money that is collected or _____ by zoo exhibits is not very much. It is greatly _____.

10. The mother elephant wasn't taking care of her young _____ very well, and it died.

11. The companionship of other female elephants will increase or _____ the mother elephant's confidence and make her feel better.

12. The director of Zoo Check Canada says that the zoo's conservation efforts deceive the public and are a _____.

> **Listening STRATEGY**
> Listen for the feelings and emotions behind the message. Understanding the emotions of the speakers can help you figure out the main ideas and how the speakers feel about them.

Listening for the Main Ideas

Listen to the interview once and answer the questions.

 **Track 88**

1. What are some of the new developments at the Calgary Zoo that are discussed in the interview?

2. Who is Rob Laidlaw and what is his general opinion of elephants in zoos?

3. What are the opposing ideas discussed in this interview?

Listening Comprehension

In the notes below, the main topics discussed in the interview are listed on the left. Some of the details about each topic are on the right.

Track 89

A. Listen to the interview as many times as necessary. As you listen, check the details and add to the notes.

Topics	Details
Significant event at Calgary Zoo	–new baby elephant was born at the zoo
Animal rights organizations	–speak on behalf of animals, especially elephants
Reactions by Rob Laidlaw, executive director of Zoo Check Canada	–not a victory for conservation
Calgary Zoo's "Elephant crossing"	–newly opened home for elephants at the zoo
Rob Laidlaw's opinion of "Elephant crossing"	–cost was very high
Rob Laidlaw's opinion of the breeding of animals in zoos	–breeding is not a sign of welfare
Calgary Zoo's plans to handle the new situation, according to spokesman Kevin Strange	–Calgary Zoo reviewed its practices or protocols
Calgary Zoo's conservation, outreach, and research program	–Calgary Zoo has a significant conservation, outreach, and research program
Rob Laidlaw's opinion of the benefits of the work of zoos in conservation and education	–the trickle-down theory of money for conservation is a theory that zoos like to talk about
Rob Laidlaw's reactions to claims made by zoos about the dangers that elephants face in the wild	–not true that elephants are shot in the wild everywhere
Zoo Check's requirements for animals in captivity	–if we have animals in captivity we need to examine their biological and behavioural needs

B. Check your notes with a partner and your teacher.

Personalizing

Work in a group of three or four. Decide which of the two opposing views about elephants or other animals in zoos your group supports. Give reasons for your decision.

VOCABULARY AND LANGUAGE CHUNKS

Write the number of each expression next to its meaning. After checking your answers, choose six expressions and write your own sentences.

Expressions	Meanings
1. the bottom line	_____ the argument is not logical, reasonable, or strong; not to make sense
2. in a perfect world	_____ growing or living in a natural state
3. at face value	_____ ability to enjoy life and to live a satisfying life
4. to buy into	_____ in a different place or location
5. in the wild	_____ very bad; extremely poor situation
6. to not hold water	_____ the way things look on the surface; superficial appearance
7. trickle-down theory	_____ to accept as true and valid
8. you can bet	_____ the idea that benefits at the top of an organization eventually reach the people at the bottom
9. a cause for celebration	_____ you can be sure, certain about
10. to be vocal	_____ a reason to be happy and to celebrate
11. off site	__1__ the most important thing or consideration
12. quality of life	_____ ideally; in the best of all possible circumstances
13. dire circumstances	_____ to speak up loudly and frequently
14. to play a part	_____ to be to someone's advantage or benefit
15. to give birth	_____ to participate in; to have something to do with
16. to work in someone's favour	_____ to bear or produce offspring or young

SPEAKING 2

Communication Focus 2: Expressing Disapproval and Criticizing

Criticizing is a strong way to express disapproval. It is used in making an argument or in simply stating strong disapproval. In casual or friendly conversation, people use more diplomatic, very indirect ways of expressing disapproval and criticizing.

Structures/Expressions	Examples
. . . to be wrong	Keeping animals in zoos is wrong.
. . . to be terrible/awful/horrible/horrendous	Wearing fur coats is horrible.
. . . shouldn't . . .	Hunters shouldn't kill baby seals.
. . . should . . .	Canada should ban seal hunting.
. . . shouldn't have (+ past participle)	The oil spill shouldn't have happened.
. . . should have (+ past participle)	The company should have been forced to clean up the oil.
. . . to be supposed to . . .	The government is supposed to protect the environment. Hunters aren't supposed to kill endangered species of animals

Grammar Note: *to be supposed to*

One of the language functions of *to be supposed to* . . . is criticizing. Please note the different structures and meanings.

Structures	Meanings	Examples
to be supposed to + base form of verb	It is expected.	You threw the bottle in the garbage, but you are supposed to put it into the recycling bin.
not to be supposed to + base form of verb	It isn't allowed.	You are not supposed to smoke near this building.
was/were supposed to + base form of the verb	It was expected to happen but did not.	They were supposed to close the elephant exhibit last year, but it's still open.
wasn't/weren't supposed to + base form of the verb	It wasn't allowed but the action was carried out.	They weren't supposed to fish in these waters, but they did it anyway.

SPEAKING ACTIVITY 3

A. On its website, the group People for the Ethical Treatment of Animals (PETA) makes the following statements. Work with a partner and make a list of as many specific things as you can think of that PETA believes people aren't supposed to do.

1. Animals are not ours to eat.
2. Animals are not ours to wear.
3. Animals are not ours to experiment on.
4. Animals are not ours to use for entertainment.
5. Animals are not ours to abuse in any way.

B. What do you and your partner disapprove of the most?

SPEAKING ACTIVITY 4

Work with a partner. Rank the environmental dangers from the most serious (1) to the least serious (10). Then join another pair and compare your answers. Report the five actions that your group criticizes the most.

_____ Burning fossil fuels such as petroleum and coal to produce energy is a common practice in all countries.

_____ Burying nuclear waste in the earth and dumping it into oceans is a common practice.

_____ Population growth: the world's population is well over 7 billion people and will be 9 billion by 2040.

_____ More and more plants and animals are becoming extinct.

_____ The release of greenhouse gases has caused the temperature to increase worldwide.

_____ Rivers, lakes, and oceans are becoming more polluted.

_____ Overfishing has greatly reduced the number of fish in the oceans.

_____ The use of cars has greatly increased all over the globe.

_____ Oil companies are building pipelines to carry oil over hundreds of miles, disturbing land, water resources, and protected areas.

_____ Oil spills have caused, and are still causing, great damage to oceans and coastal areas, and to the birds, fish, and animals which live in them.

Communication Focus 3: Expressing Opinions with Various Degrees of Certainty

A. When we express opinions we often begin with one of these phrases:

I think/feel/believe . . .   I'd like to say/point out . . .

In my opinion . . .   If you ask me . . .

B. When we are very certain that we are right we can use one of these stronger expressions:

I'm certain/sure/positive that . . .   There's no question in my mind
                                          that . . .

I honestly believe/feel/think . . .   In my (honest) opinion . . .

I am convinced that . . .

C. When we are unsure or want to be polite or diplomatic we can use one of these milder phrases:

It seems to me . . .   As far as I know . . .

I imagine . . .   People say . . .

Responses to Opinions

Less Certain/Neutral	Strong Agreement	Strong Disagreement
I suppose so/not.	Absolutely!	Absolutely not!
I guess you're right.	You're absolutely right!	I totally disagree.
If you think so.	No question about it!	I'm convinced that's not true/right.
Really?	I couldn't agree more.	Are you kidding?
	You're right! Right on!	No way!

👥 SPEAKING ACTIVITY 5

Work in a group of four. Find out how everyone feels about the following issues. Use expressions that show how strongly you feel. Report to the class.

1. In your opinion, what are some of the worst things people have done to wild animals?

2. Do you think pets should be treated like people? For example, North Americans spend over 40 billion dollars on their pets each year. What's your opinion of this?

3. Do you believe animals can communicate? Explain why.

4. What do you think animals might say about humans if they could communicate?

5. Do you think animals should have rights? Please explain.

6. What can humans learn from animals?

7. Do you think some animals can think and can express their feelings? Please explain.

8. What, in your opinion, are some differences between people and animals? Please explain.

9. What different views of animals are there in other countries and cultures? For example, in North America a dog is considered a

person's best friend, whereas in some countries dogs are thought to be very low, dirty animals.

10. Which of the following do you believe exist? Please explain.

   a. vampires

   b. werewolves

   c. mermaids

   d. the Loch Ness Monster

   e. Bigfoot (also known as Sasquatch, a huge apelike creature which is said to inhabit mountain forests)

   f. other unusual creatures

👥 SPEAKING ACTIVITY 6

Here is a *true/false* quiz about the human animal and the differences between the sexes. Complete the quiz with a partner. State your opinions. Compare your answers with the answers of another pair of students and discuss your differences. The teacher will give you the answers which are based on research findings. What surprised you the most?

Statements	True	False
1. Women have a greater capacity for feeling happy than men do.		
2. Women are better at learning and using language than men are.		
3. Men are more accurate at throwing or catching objects than women.		
4. Women are more talkative and communicative than men.		
5. Women have more trouble reading maps than men.		
6. Men are better at mathematics than women.		
7. Men and women have different approaches to problem solving.		
8. Men and women have different kinds of dreams.		
9. Men lie more often than women.		
10. In stressful situations, men and women respond very differently.		

Communication Focus 4: Expressing Regrets

We can express regrets about our own actions or about situations in general. We can use a variety of structures to express regret.

Structures/Expressions	Examples
It's too bad . . .	It's too bad that cars pollute the environment so much.
I (really) regret . . .	I really regret buying a car.
I'm sorry that (about) . . .	I'm sorry that everyone wants to drive a car.
I wish . . .	I wish people could get along without cars.

Grammar Note: Using *wish* to Refer to Present, Past, and Future Time

When we use *wish* to express regrets, we are talking about situations which are contrary to fact.

Present Time

Structure	Examples
. . . *wish* + past form	I wish I didn't need to drive to work (but I do).
	I wish I lived closer to work (but I don't).
	I wish I could walk to work (but I can't).
	I wish I were closer to work (but I am not).

Past Time

Structure	Examples
. . . *wish* + past perfect	Monica wishes she hadn't had to drive to school last year (but she did).
	She wishes she had walked to school (but she didn't).

Future Time

Structure	Examples
. . . *wish* + *would*	I wish people would stop producing so much garbage (but I don't think they will).

SPEAKING ACTIVITY 7

Work with a partner. Use *wish* to make statements about the following. Compare your answers with another pair of students and report the most interesting ideas to the class.

Example:

> **I wish the population of the world weren't so large. I wish there were fewer people in the world.**

1. The world population is over 7 billion people.
2. Global warming is melting the ice in the Arctic and Antarctic regions.
3. There are serious shortages of water. Pollution of rivers, lakes, and groundwater limits the supply even more.
4. There is a shortage of some kinds of fish due to overfishing, and large areas of the ocean are so polluted that they are now dead zones.

5. Tropical rain forests, as well as temperate forests, are being destroyed rapidly. Some forest types will be gone in a few years and most by the end of the century.

6. Worldwide demand for gasoline leads oil companies to drill for oil and build pipelines, and this can result in horrible damages from oil spills.

7. Other important issue/concern: _____

Speaking STRATEGY

People often start conversations by mentioning something that they heard, something they read about, or something in the news. This is a good strategy to start a conversation.

SPEAKING ACTIVITY 8

Work with a partner. What are some personal regrets you have about yourself?

Regrets	Me	My Partner
In what ways do you wish you were different?		
Where do you wish you lived?		
What do you wish you did for a living?		
How many languages do you wish you spoke?		
What do you wish you could do?		
How much money do you wish you had?		
What do you wish you didn't have to do?		
What is a regret you have about something you did in the past?		
What is a regret you have about something you didn't do in the past?		

Communication Focus 5: Hypothesizing

When we hypothesize, we assume or suppose something will happen if certain conditions exist. We use conditional sentences referring to the future, to the present, or to the past to hypothesize.

Hypothesizing about the . . .	Structures/Expressions	Examples
Future	*If* + present tense, . . . *will* + base form of verb	**If** there **are** too many people on earth, there **will not be** enough food to feed everyone.
	Suppose + present tense, . . . *will* + base form of the verb	**Suppose** the world population **continues** to grow, **will** there **be** enough food?
Present	*If* + past tense, . . . *would* + base form of the verb	**If** 10 billion people **inhabited** the planet, there **would be** many environmental problems. If we **could control** population growth, the earth **wouldn't become** overcrowded.
	Suppose + past tense, . . . *would* + base form of the verb	**Suppose** the earth **became** overcrowded, **would** people **begin** to colonize the moon?
Past	*If* + past perfect tense, . . . *would have* + past participle	**If** they **hadn't cut** down the rain forests in that part of Brazil, they **wouldn't have had** enough farmland to grow food.

SPEAKING ACTIVITY 9

Work with a partner and interview him or her. Hypothesize about these situations.

1. If you could live anywhere in the world, where would you live?
2. If you could make one change to the environment, what change would you make?
3. If you could change one thing about yourself, what would you change?
4. If you had been born in North America, how would your life have been different?
5. If you won a lottery which made you rich beyond your wildest dreams, which friends would you stay close to and what would you do?
6. If you could change places with someone for a month, who would you change places with and why?
7. If you could have three wishes, what would you ask for?
8. If you had been able to choose any time in history to live in, which period would you have chosen?
9. If you hadn't come to this country, what would you have done?
10. What things would you do if you had only six months to live?

LISTENING 2: THE EFFECTS OF CLIMATE CHANGE ON THE FOOD SUPPLY— A DOCUMENTARY REPORT

Before You Listen

👥 Pre-listening Activity

Work in a small group. Discuss the following questions.

1. What is a refugee?
2. What different kinds of refugees have you heard of?
3. How many refugees are there in the world today?
4. How do you think the refugee situation in the world will change in the future?

👥 Pre-listening Vocabulary

A. You will hear a report on the audio CD that includes the following vocabulary. Work with a partner or by yourself to write the correct word next to its definition in the chart below.

migration	intense	drought	to decline
to afflict	dispute	desertification	affordable
runaway	to flee	emissions	fossil fuels
correspondent	death toll	equator	border
to fortify	advance guard	obvious	adequate
non-negotiable	implication	impact	to collapse
defence	doable	hurricane	greenhouse gases
irreversible	intervention	crude	

Definitions	Vocabulary
1. to strengthen	to fortify
2. very strong; extreme	
3. a strong effect on someone or something	
4. something that is suggested or implied	
5. argument; disagreement	
6. clear; easily seen; self-evident	
7. the number of deaths	
8. troops or soldiers sent ahead of the main army	
9. of low cost; can be afforded	
10. a long period of dry weather with no rain	

continued on next page

Definitions	Vocabulary
11. severe tropical storm with winds above 75 miles per hour	
12. imaginary circle around the widest part of the earth an equal distance from both poles	
13. organic substances such as oil, gas, and coal used to produce energy or heat	
14. to grow worse in condition; to decrease, to become less	
15. to break down in strength; to fall apart	
16. something that has escaped control	
17. act of moving from one region to another	
18. able to be done	
19. transformation or change of farming land to desert	
20. incapable of being turned back; cannot be reversed	
21. person who communicates by writing or reporting	
22. to cause pain or suffering	
23. to escape from	
24. protection, defending against attack	
25. not open to change or discussion	
26. not very sophisticated, basic, simple	
27. the act of coming between two things for a purpose	
28. an imaginary line separating two countries	
29. enough for a specific requirement; satisfactory or acceptable	
30. release of certain gases	
31. gases that trap and hold heat in the upper atmosphere	

B. Choose the correct vocabulary from the list above to fill in the blanks in these sentences. Use each word only once. Not all the words are used in the sentences. Please make changes to verbs or nouns when necessary.

1. In times of war, countries _____fortify_____ their borders.

2. Many people believe that the release or _____ of _____ are responsible for global warming.

3. Climatologists predict that as the earth grows warmer there will be water shortages and an increase in the size of deserts or _____ in countries close to the _____, and the people won't be able to grow crops there.

4. The result of using _____ to produce heat and energy is damage to the earth's ozone layer.

5. The newspaper said that as global warming became worse the US military would forget about _____ or wars in foreign countries and would bring their troops home.

6. The numbers who died or the _____ _____ from the hurricane was several hundred people.

7. As global warming increases many refugees will _____ to countries with lower temperatures.

8. Paty Romero Lankao is a sociologist who studies the _____ or possible effects of global warming and the effects or _____ it will have on populations.

9. Climate predictions say that Mexico and Central America will _____ with severe _____ because of lack of rain.

10. Once world temperatures have risen by over five percent, climate change will be _____ _____.

11. Problems with their food supply caused many civilizations _____ and _____.

12. Just because something is _____ does not mean that it will be done.

13. There will be _____ global warming if governments don't take any action to control it.

Listening STRATEGY 🎧

An important strategy for comprehending listening texts is to have an overall understanding of the background and the context of the listening. Try to understand the context of the listening and you will understand the main ideas better.

Listening for the Main Ideas

Background Information

Gwynne Dyer is a Canadian journalist who wrote a book and did a radio series called *Climate Wars*, both of which are about the geopolitics of climate change. The report you are going to hear is part of the second report of the series.

 **Track 90**

Listen to the report once and then answer the questions.

1. What crisis does this program describe?
2. What is causing this crisis?
3. In what ways are some countries reacting to the crisis?
4. What is the overall tone of the report? Why do you feel that way?

Listening Comprehension

In the notes below, the main points discussed appear on the left. Some of the details about each point are on the right.

 **Track 91**

A. Listen to the report again. As you listen, check the details and add any information that is missing. You may want to listen several times.

Main Points	Details
Gwynne Dyer's first experience with climate refugees	–three times during 10 days, boats full of refugees sailed onto the tourist beaches in Tenerife, Canary Islands
Where the climate refugees come from	–40,000 went to the European Union the year before this report
The predicted effects of global warming on the earth	–desertification to the south of the US, in Mexico, and in Central America
Michael Klare	–professor of Peace and World Security Studies at Hampshire College in Amherst, Massachusetts
The US reaction to climate refugees, according to Michael Klare	–when hundreds of millions of refugees travel north, the US will fortify the US–Mexican border
What the destination countries are doing to stop climate refugees	–European Union has naval patrols to turn them back and they try to bribe their countries of origin to stop the refugees from leaving
IPCC	–international body under the United Nations
Climate predictions	–200 million people in Mexico, Central America, and the Caribbean

The pattern Gwynne Dyer sees in the effects of global warming	–your most dangerous neighbour is the one who lies between you and the equator
Lester Brown and his opinions about the food supply	–grand old man of the environmental movement
Why Gwynne Dyer thinks we are lucky	–if the crisis had happened 50 years earlier, there would have been no major alternative
Gwynne Dyer's conclusions about global warming	–we have the technology to stop global warming

B. Check your notes with a partner and your teacher.

Personalizing

Work in a group of three or four. These are some quotations from the report. Discuss them and try to reach consensus about whether your group agrees with them or not. Try to persuade the others whose opinions are different from yours.

1. The migration of climate refugees could "change the face of the planet."

2. "The crude formula is: 'Your most dangerous neighbour is the one who lies between you and the equator.'"

3. "But the fact that it's doable does not mean that it [controlling climate change] will be done."

4. "Some people think it's too late already [to stop climate change]. Others think we might have 10 years."

VOCABULARY AND LANGUAGE CHUNKS

Write the number of each expression next to its meaning. After checking your answers, choose six expressions and write your own sentences.

Expressions	Meanings
1. to go on	_____ to prosper, to succeed; to benefit from
2. to do quite well	_____ to change the appearance of something completely
3. out of control	__1__ to continue
4. to change the face of something	_____ for us; on our part
5. to come off better	_____ to wait before acting
6. weak link	_____ to turn out; to result; to become
7. on our behalf	_____ to lose a great deal
8. to hold off	_____ the weakest; the least dependable element
9. to take a big hit	_____ to do the correct thing; to do something the correct way
10. to end up	_____ not able to be controlled
11. to get it right	_____ to have a better-than-expected outcome
12. to run into trouble	_____ to come to an end; to be used up
13. to get something done	_____ to start to have problems or difficulties
14. to run out	_____ to deal playfully or not seriously with
15. to flirt with	_____ to do something; to finish something

PRONUNCIATION

Pronunciation Focus 1: Non-final Intonation and Final Intonation

 Track 92

As we saw in previous chapters, intonation involves the rise and fall of the voice. Intonation patterns are essential for understanding if the speaker has finished speaking or still has more to say. If the speaker has finished, the voice rises and then falls to its lowest pitch level on the last stressed syllable of the last word. If the speaker hasn't finished speaking, the voice rises slightly and levels off without falling.

PRONUNCIATION ACTIVITY 1

Listen to these sentences:

1. Those people are refugees.

2. If a person is a refugee, he or she is protected by many governments.

3. Human rights are important in modern society.

4. If human rights are important, we need to protect them.

In the first and third examples, the speaker's voice falls at the end of the sentences. In the second and fourth examples, the speaker's voice levels off but the pitch does not fall at the end of the first clause. This shows that the speaker still has more to say and is not finished.

PRONUNCIATION ACTIVITY 2

A. Listen to the sentences and circle **Finished** if the voice drops and **Not Finished** if the voice levels off or rises slightly and does not drop.

 Track 93

1. If you are worried about climate change	Finished	(Not Finished)
2. Some people say we still have 10 years	Finished	Not Finished
3. It's too late already	Finished	Not Finished
4. Your most dangerous neighbour	Finished	Not Finished
5. Britain became the world's richest country and dominated the world	Finished	Not Finished
6. Since these people are moving from poor countries to richer ones	Finished	Not Finished
7. As the warming proceeds	Finished	Not Finished
8. The destination countries are already taking defensive measures	Finished	Not Finished
9. They will follow the well-beaten path and	Finished	Not Finished
10. If all the ice melts in the Arctic	Finished	Not Finished
11. Due to overfishing there has been a reduction of fish stocks	Finished	Not Finished
12. Once the climate warms up three or four degrees	Finished	Not Finished
13. In the Arctic, seals are hunted for their fur and meat	Finished	Not Finished
14. As soon as North America runs out of water	Finished	Not Finished

B. Write an ending to those sentences above which have non-final intonation and practise saying all the sentences with a partner.

Pronunciation Focus 2: Indicating Choices

 Track 94   In English, we use certain intonation patterns to indicate choices.

 PRONUNCIATION ACTIVITY 3

A. Intonation can signal choices. Listen to the sentences. Draw rising arrows where the voice rises or levels off and falling arrows where the voice falls.

1. Do you want to see a movie about global warming or about refugees?
2. Will the earth's temperature rise by two degrees or five degrees?
3. Would you rather live in the city or the country?
4. Should we ride bicycles or drive cars?
5. Which do you want to hear first—the bad news or the good news?

B. What is the intonation pattern when there is a choice? Check your work with the class and the teacher.

PRONUNCIATION ACTIVITY 4

Track 95   A. Repeat these sentences.

1. Would you rather be wise or wealthy?
2. Should we go to a concert or to the theatre?
3. Would you like a glass of wine or some beer?
4. Do you want to work in a small company or a large one?
5. Which do you like better, the book or the movie?
6. Did you say it was 10:50 or 10:15?
7. Which would you rather visit, California or Hawaii?
8. Do you feel like walking or driving?
9. Would you rather marry for love or for money?
10. Who do you think is more handsome, Brad Pitt or George Clooney?

B. Work with a partner and write five original sentences which you can ask two other pairs of students. Report to the class about how you did.

Your sentences:

1. _____
2. _____
3. _____
4. _____
5. _____

Pronunciation Focus 3: Lists

In English, there is a specific intonation pattern for lists.

 **Track 96**

 PRONUNCIATION ACTIVITY 5

Listen to the sentences and draw rising arrows where the voice rises and falling arrows where the voice falls. Then check your answers with the teacher and the class.

1. She visited Asia, Africa, South America, and Australia.
2. We want to learn the forms, the meanings, and the uses of the modals.
3. They've bought furniture, appliances, carpets, and plants for their new house.

 PRONUNCIATION ACTIVITY 6

A. Work with a partner and predict the intonation pattern on the following sentences.

 **Track 97**

   1. Helen wants to study mathematics, physics, chemistry, and biology at university.
   2. Andrea bought new scarves, purses, gloves, and jewellery.
   3. We need potatoes, carrots, spinach, broccoli, and lettuce.
   4. I'd love to visit Argentina, Brazil, Peru, and Uruguay next year.
   5. John has never liked soccer, baseball, hockey, or basketball.

B. Listen to the sentences to check your answers.
C. Practise saying the sentences to each other.

PRONUNCIATION ACTIVITY 7

This is a game to practise intonation with lists. Work in a group of four or five. One person will be the scorekeeper. He/she will throw a die to determine the subject, according to the following chart. Then students throw the die to determine who goes first, second, etc. The first player must state two items from the category. For example, if the number thrown by the scorekeeper is 4, the category is fruit, so the first player will make up a sentence that includes two fruits. The next player will repeat the sentences with the first two items and add the name of another fruit, and so on.

Example:

> Student 1: I went to the store and bought apples and bananas.
>
> Student 2: I went to the store and bought apples, bananas, and oranges.

The group scores a point for each word in the category. When the group cannot think of any other words to add, they can choose a new category by rolling the die again. After 10 or so minutes of play, the group with the highest total points wins.

Number on the Die	Categories	Points
1	cities you want to visit	
2	countries you want to see	
3	vegetables	
4	fruit	
5	stores or businesses	
6	languages	

Some other categories for Round 2 of this game could be sports, actors, colours, animals, how to be a successful student, and how to make friends.

COMMUNICATING IN THE REAL WORLD

Use your English to talk to people outside your classroom. On your own or with a partner, talk to five people outside your class. Make up your own questions based on the topics in this chapter or ask the questions below and record the information.

Make a short report to the class about what you learned.

Here is one way to introduce your assignment.

Could I ask you some questions? I am doing an assignment for my English class.

1. How do you think our children's lives will be different as a result of what our generation has done to the environment?

2. What do you think are some of the worst environmental crimes or damages?

3. What, in your opinion, are some of the worst things people have done to animals?

4. What do you think of having animals in circuses, zoos, or aquariums?

5. What can we humans learn from animals?

6. Who do you think is better, generally, at learning and using language—men or women?

7. What in your opinion should be done about traffic and the number of cars on the roads in this city?

8. In what ways do you wish you were different?

9. What do you wish you had or hadn't done in the past?

10. If you won a lottery that made you very rich, what you do?

SELF-EVALUATION

Think about your work in this chapter. For each row in the chart sections **Grammar and Language Functions**, **Language Strategies**, and **Pronunciation**, give yourself a score based on the rating scale below and write a comment in the Notes section.

Show the chart to your teacher. Talk about what you need to do to make your English better.

Rating Scale

1	2	3	4	5

Needs improvement. ← → *Great!*

	Score	Notes
Grammar and Language Functions		
using the passive voice to ask for and give impersonal information		
expressing disapproval and criticizing		
expressing opinions with various degrees of certainty		
expressing regrets		
hypothesizing		
Pronunciation		
using final and non-final intonation		
using intonation to signal choices		
using intonation with lists		

Learning Strategies

Speaking

taking a chance and trying to express my ideas if I have something to say (not worrying about sounding foolish or making mistakes)		
starting conversations by mentioning something I have heard or read about, or something in the news		

Listening

listening for the feelings and emotions of the speaker to help me figure out the main ideas		
trying to get an overall understanding of the background and the context of the listening to better understand the main ideas		

Vocabulary and Language Chunks

Look at the list of new vocabulary and language chunks you learned in this chapter. Give yourself a score based on the rating scale and write a comment.

to go on	to get it right	the bottom line
to do quite well	to run into trouble	in a perfect world
out of control	to get something done	at face value
to end up	in time	to buy into
to change the face of something	to run out	in the wild
to come off better	to take a big hit	not to hold water
weak link	to be vocal	trickle-down theory
on our behalf	quality of life	you can bet
to hold off	dire circumstances	a cause for celebration
to take a big hit	to play a part	to work in someone's favour
	to give birth	

	Score	Notes
understanding new vocabulary and language chunks		
using new words and phrases correctly		

Write eight sentences and use new vocabulary you learned in this chapter.

1. _____
2. _____
3. _____
4. _____
5. _____
6. _____
7. _____
8. _____

My plan for practising is

_____

_____

_____

_____

APPENDIX

Irregular Verbs

A. These irregular verbs don't follow a specific rule in forming the simple past and past participle. The forms need to be memorized.

Base Form	Simple Past	Past Participle
be	was, were	been
beat	beat	beaten
bite	bit	bitten
break	broke	broken
choose	chose	chosen
do	did	done
fly	flew	flown
forget	forgot	forgotten
freeze	froze	frozen
get	got	got (gotten)
go	went	gone
lie	lay	lain
read	read	read
ride	rode	ridden
speak	spoke	spoken
steal	stole	stolen
tear	tore	torn
write	wrote	written
wake	woke	woken

B. The following five types of irregular verbs follow specific patterns in forming the past and the past participle.

Group 1

All three verb forms are the same.

Base Form	Simple Past	Past Participle
bet	bet	bet
cost	cost	cost
cut	cut	cut
fit	fit	fit
hit	hit	hit
hurt	hurt	hurt
let	let	let
put	put	put
quit	quit	quit
shut	shut	shut
spread	spread	spread

Group 2

In these verbs, the form for the past and the past participle is the same.

Base Form	Simple Past	Past Participle
bring	brought	brought
build	built	built
buy	bought	bought
catch	caught	caught
feed	fed	fed
feel	felt	felt
fight	fought	fought
find	found	found
hang	hung	hung
have	had	had
hear	heard	heard
hold	held	held
keep	kept	kept
kneel	knelt	knelt
lay	laid	laid
lead	led	led
leave	left	left
lend	lent	lent
lose	lost	lost
make	made	made
mean	meant	meant
meet	met	met
pay	paid	paid
say	said	said
sell	sold	sold
send	sent	sent
shine	shone	shone
shoot	shot	shot
sit	sat	sat
sleep	slept	slept
spend	spent	spent
stand	stood	stood
strike	struck	struck
teach	taught	taught
tell	told	told
think	thought	thought
understand	understood	understood

Credits

Group 3

In these verbs, the vowels change from *i* in the present to *a* in the past and *u* in the past participle.

Base Form	Simple Past	Past Participle
begin	began	begun
drink	drank	drunk
ring	rang	rung
shrink	shrank	shrunk
sing	sang	sung
sink	sank	sunk
swim	swam	swum

Group 4

In these verbs, the past participle is the same as the base form, but we add *-n* or *-en* to the past participle.

Base Form	Simple Past	Past Participle
blow	blew	blown
draw	drew	drawn
drive	drove	driven
eat	ate	eaten
fall	fell	fallen
give	gave	given
grow	grew	grown
hide	hid	hidden
know	knew	known
shake	shook	shaken
take	took	taken
throw	threw	thrown

Group 5

In these verbs, the past participle is the same as the base form of the verb.

Base Form	Simple Past	Past Participle
become	became	become
come	came	come
run	ran	run

CREDITS

Photo and Figure Credits